D1474723

IT'S HARD TO TALK ABOUT YOURSELF

NATALIA GINZBURG

IT'S HARD TO TALK ABOUT YOURSELF

EDITED BY CESARE GARBOLI AND LISA GINZBURG
TRANSLATED BY LOUISE QUIRKE

THE UNIVERSITY OF CHICAGO PRESS

CHICAGO AND LONDON

NATALIA GINZBURG (1916–1991) WROTE NOVELS, SHORT STORIES, POEMS, PLAYS, AND ESSAY AND TRANSLATED PROUST AND FLAUBERT. AMONG HER MANY BOOKS ARE *THE ROAD TO THE CITY: TWO NOVELLAS* (1942), *VALENTINO* (1957), *FAMILY SAYINGS* (1963), *NEVER MUST YOU ASK ME* (1970), AND *THE MANZONI FAMILY* (1983).

LOUISE QUIRKE IS A PROFESSIONAL TRANSLATOR WHO HAS WORKED FOR EDITORI LATERZA AND CAMBRIDGE UNIVERSITY PRESS.

THE UNIVERSITY OF CHICAGO PRESS, CHICAGO 60637
THE UNIVERSITY OF CHICAGO PRESS, LTD., LONDON
© 2003 BY THE UNIVERSITY OF CHICAGO
ALL RIGHTS RESERVED. PUBLISHED 2003
PRINTED IN THE UNITED STATES OF AMERICA
12 11 10 09 08 07 06 05 04 03   1 2 3 4 5
ISBN: 0-226-29688-1 (CLOTH)

ORIGINALLY PUBLISHED AS *É DIFFICILE PARLARE DI SÉ*.
© 1999 GIULIO EINAUDI EDITORE S.P.A., TURIN.

LIBRARY OF CONGRESS CATALOGING-IN-PUBLICATION DATA

GINZBURG, NATALIA.
  [É DIFFICILE PARLARE DI SÉ. ENGLISH]
  IT'S HARD TO TALK ABOUT YOURSELF / NATALIA GINZBURG ; EDITED BY CESARE GARBOLI AND LISA GINZBURG ; TRANSLATED BY LOUISE QUIRKE.
    P.   CM.
  TEXTS OF CONVERSATIONS, CONDUCTED BY MARINO SINIBALDI, FROM THE RADIO PROGRAM ANTOLOGIA, TRANSMITTED ON RADIO TRE DURING FOUR CONSECUTIVE SUNDAYS IN MAY, 1990.
  INCLUDES INDEX.
  ISBN 0-226-29688-1 (CLOTH : ALK. PAPER)
  1. GINZBURG, NATALIA—INTERVIEWS. 2. AUTHORS, ITALIAN—20TH CENTURY—INTERVIEWS. I. GARBOLI, CESARE. II. GINZBURG, LISA. III. SINIBALDI, MARINO. IV. ANTOLOGIA (RADIO PROGRAM) V. TITLE.
  PQ4817.I5 Z463513   2003
  853'.912—DC21   2002153254

♾ THE PAPER USED IN THIS PUBLICATION MEETS THE MINIMUM REQUIREMENTS OF THE AMERICAN NATIONAL STANDARD FOR INFORMATION SCIENCES—PERMANENCE OF PAPER FOR PRINTED LIBRARY MATERIALS, ANSI Z39.48–1992.

CONTENTS

PREFACE

I remember two phone calls from my grandmother. On both occasions it was a Sunday evening (in spring: I can still see the golden light in the apartment while I talk on the phone). She was calling after two long conversations with Marino Sinibaldi, which had been recorded for a radio program about her and which are now being published in this book.

She was tired, she said, but happy. "It's hard to talk about yourself, but good, too," she told me. As for the second call, I remember a particularly sad note to her voice. She felt a little exposed, and this came across clearly in what she said.

There was a constant conflict in her between a part that was carefree and liked to dream and one that was firmly and constantly anchored to reality. I believe that in this contrast lies one of the deepest roots of her vocation as a writer. I have often wondered whether the second part, the more pragmatic one, had not developed more than it would otherwise have done, a necessary consequence of the tragedies that struck in the course of her life. There was a lightness that shone in her eyes even though her ways were often rigid and always sober and austere. It was a lightness that events had suffocated but the memory of which she hung onto with happiness and gratitude. I think of it as I remember how sometimes her face would relax into an open, carefree smile, offering to whomever happened to be near the kind of warmth of an unexpected embrace; I think of it as I remember how she could really laugh in a completely uninhibited way. When you were near her, you felt yourself immersed in a universe where the rules of the world could somehow be carried along by an airy freedom, by a breath that always managed to last longer than events.

But she had learned the laws of reality. She tried (and she did so with great energy, always shunning pretence) not to tell herself lies, always to look on the world through lucid eyes. She was never cynical but saw through things, never emphatic but always passionate, ready to catch what caught her attention more than anything else: the story of events in human lives. She could be wrong at times, she could have opinions that were at times very extreme, but her energy, her tension was constantly turned toward reality in an attempt to understand the world by reducing it to a few elements that always had something outstanding for whoever was listening: because they were simple elements, original, linked to life. Familiar images that anyone can understand because they bring with them always the comfort that comes from their very simplicity and universality. That is, things became clearer when they were close to her; they came across more authentically and more comprehensibly because she forced herself to see them for what they were, without coloring them.

The rare occasions when I go to see her at the cemetery invariably follow the same pattern. Once inside I start looking urgently for the place: I can't find it, and I start walking round in an aimless fashion. Eventually I find it, but only after having wandered around for some time feeling vaguely anxious but also aware of a profound sense of peace. It is strange how these two states of mind mix, to be followed by an almost fatal sense that takes over, a premonition that sooner or later I will get to the right place, the place where she is buried. And sure enough, I get there, I put the water and flowers in a metal vase, and then I stay just for a moment to greet her, perhaps to tell her the important things that have happened.

That sense of premonition I have until I find the place where she is, that intense awareness of an inevitability strong enough to dominate the shadow of a doubt running alongside it with the promise of something more serene: these combined have the power of a feeling. A feeling, which in that place that houses and evokes dead people, seems to me to be the one most alive. It is a feeling, also, that resembles her because it combines close scrutiny of the anguish and troubles that accompany every person's journey with the awareness of how much any journey needs also great peace if it is to acquire any meaning. In a short essay on translating, she wrote about the horse's pace and the ant's pace and on the importance of using both. But the same criterion—of a constant integration of swiftness into slowness, of the rapidity of creative angst being absorbed into the measured pace of the form of expression—presided over the very meaning of her life. The capacity to bear her own anxiety by having in her mind always an aspiration to serenity was uniquely hers (and I think that only toward the end of her life did she become aware of how much so). She had the ability to suffer knowing that there is no true cure for pain but that there must inevitably be a period of quiet to go with the storms in order to express that pain.

There was a silence in her, a deep and intimate silence (recently, in different ways, her friends Dinda Gallo and Vittorio Foa have spoken to me about it, and it is possible, at least for people who knew her, to pick it up also in the course of the conversations that comprise this book). In the noise of her very active days you could hear the echo of the solitary hours at dawn spent writing, stealing time from sleep to obey what she herself called her "master": the vital, unquestionable, and absolute need to give time to her writing. It was an internal silence that you could read in her face, in the way she would half-shut her eyes, absorbed in the effort of listening carefully to what was going on around her, listening so that later she could "chew it over." The "ruminating" of thoughts was an idea of which she was particularly fond, the same one she used to defend her periods of sheer idleness. This idleness is useful, she would say, because only when we are idle does the mind "ruminate." But her silence was far from idle; rather, it galloped along, light and full of thought. It was a silence in which she would always manage to find a voice so that she could describe and comment on the world's happenings or on books she had read and films she had seen with a judgment that was entirely her own. This independence she would protect with strenuous and sometimes fiery efforts: she was as sure and steadfast in her opinions as someone can be only if their strength comes from having listened to their own voice in silence.

Working on these interviews together with Cesare Garboli, my grandmother's dearest friend, has been moving, painful, and exciting. This is how life always seemed to me when I was around my grandmother. Painful and exciting. That's why she loved Chekhov so much—toward the end of her life she would often say that, because in Chekhov, in his plays and stories, she found bundled together pain and pleasure, melancholia and life, the violence of passions and the gentleness of feelings. It was this amalgamating of things, this mixing of vital and torpid elements, of tragedies and great consolations, which was an inspiration to her and caused her constantly to reflect, even when she seemed to be intent on other things. She thought about it and fed on it for her writing.

Having been granted the gift of her love and friendship, it is with a great and sharp sense of loss that I remember her. I can see now the look of total absorption that would come into her eyes as she sat on her long blue sofa, smoking and talking or just being quiet, listening, understanding (and she understands because she feels and because later on she will write); with this image of her, anyone who has loved her, loved her deeply, tries to fill the sad and silent void left by her sudden death, which the text of these recorded conversations can fill only for a moment.

Lisa Ginzburg

NOTE TO THE ENGLISH EDITION

In May 1990, over four consecutive Sundays, Natalia Ginzburg took part in a series of broadcasts for the *Anthology* program on Radio Tre. Produced by Mirella Fulvi and presented by Marino Sinibaldi, the program generally took the form of long conversations between an author and various critics and guests. During the Sundays dedicated to Natalia Ginzburg, the following guests took part: Cesare Garboli, Giulio Einaudi, Masolino D'Amico, Enzo Siciliano, Guido Fink, Dinda Gallo, and Vittorio Foa. The Italian edition reproduces the text of the broadcasts exactly as they were recorded in the Rai (major Italian TV and radio network) studios. The English-language edition has been lightly edited for the Anglophone reader.

   When an excerpt has been taken from a published English-language edition, it is noted at first occurrence. Translations of works not cited at their first appearance are original to this edition.

ONE

FROM TURATI TO GINZBURG

MARINO SINIBALDI In *The Things We Used to Say* there is a description of a visit from Filippo Turati,[1] who fled Italy in 1926. You remember that episode very clearly:

> My father used to say that Turati was naïve, and my mother, who did not see naivety as a fault, would nod and sigh and say, "My poor little Filippo." Turati once came to our house, when he was passing through Turin, and I remember him in our sitting room, as large as a bear, with his gray beard closely trimmed. I met him twice, then and later on when he had to flee the country and stayed with us in hiding for a week. However, I cannot remember a single word he said that day in our sitting room. I remember a great deal of talk and discussion, and that's all.[2]

Was a visit from Turati so routine? Was it a part of the backdrop, the way of life in your house as seen through your eyes as a child?

NATALIA GINZBURG Yes, at the time it all seemed totally run-of-the-mill to me.

SINIBALDI And normal.

GINZBURG More or less, yes. But in my memory, after a few months had passed, this figure of Turati had made a big impression on me. I envisioned myself writing a book called *The Secret* and on the cover there was the figure of a child, which was me, with an enormous key in her hand, . . .

SINIBALDI And about this secret . . .

GINZBURG . . . and I knew there was a secret that I had to keep, that had to be kept quiet.

SINIBALDI A historic episode: Turati's flight from Italy in December 1926 with the help of Parri,[3] Rosselli,[4] Pertini,[5] and Adriano Olivetti.[6] An episode that sums up Turin in that period. Perhaps as in few other Italian cities of the time there was this culture emerging, the culture of Justice and Liberty,[7] with its connotations of youthful boldness, of irreverence. Weren't these the same traits that characterized the start of the anti-Fascist culture in Turin, which was just getting going? The laughing eyes of Adriano Olivetti sum it up . . .

GINZBURG Yes, but I noticed after that a great difference between Socialism—the old-style Socialism of my father, mother, and the Carrara family, whom at the time we saw a lot of—and the form that was to become true anti-Fascism, the militant variety, which I saw later in Leone Ginzburg,[8] in Vittorio Foa.[9] I saw how it was different: you see, my father was an old-style Socialist but, well, he had no idea how to oppose Fascism.

SINIBALDI But this impotence was typical of the crisis in old-style Socialism, wasn't it?

GINZBURG Yes, yes, and an absolute pessimism. "There's nothing to do, we can't get out of this now, we can't get out of this," my father would say. My mother would go to the shops and come home saying, "My greengrocer said this can't go on much longer, that Fascism will end soon." She was more optimistic. Anyway, I later understood that there were those who were trying to do something, who wrote articles for Justice and Liberty, that there was an active anti-Fascism. One of my younger brother's friends was Pajetta.[10] Pajetta was a Communist. My father didn't know any Communists but he didn't trust them and, well, this Pajetta seemed to him to be a reckless kid. You see, for him Communists weren't . . .

SINIBALDI This small world of anti-Fascists who seemed to you to be a big world—it seemed like the whole world, didn't it?

GINZBURG Well, yes, it seemed like the whole world. But then there was this big event that really surprised me because my brother Mario would argue with my father. They would talk about politics, and they would argue, and I thought that Mario was anti-Socialist, or I had got it into my head that he was not a true anti-Fascist. Then it turned out that he had become friends with—

SINIBALDI He was plotting.

GINZBURG —friends with Leone Ginzburg, and he was plotting, yes.

SINIBALDI And this was the surprise.

GINZBURG Well, it was strange, because this brother of mine, apart from the fact that he argued with my father, seemed to be interested only in shirts.

SINIBALDI And he would read that *Grandi Firme* review so disapproved of by the family.

GINZBURG [*She laughs*] It was Alberto who read that.

SINIBALDI The striking thing—and that is why I was asking whether this small world was for you the whole world—is that Fascism never figures [in your work—*trans.*].

GINZBURG Well, perhaps I never wrote about it, and I have very vague memories, but I remember that Fascism frightened me, and I think it frightened me because of what I heard my parents saying, that the Fascists could come, especially at the start, that they were killing people, burning houses. They burned down the trade union headquarters.

SINIBALDI Yes, in Turin.

GINZBURG So it was at the root of a fear that perhaps over the years I have pushed aside, but early on I felt it. It was something frightening. Then my father would speak his mind. He wasn't at all cautious, he would say things that I think were dangerous, say them in public, then he would come home and say, "Well, they were rude to me," or something, and my mother was afraid. I remember there was one man who said to him, "I'll make sure you get what's coming to you," and this really frightened my mother and me, this person who said, "I'll make sure you get what's coming to you." And my mother would say, "Oh God, oh God, who knows what they'll do to him now."

MIRELLA FULVI So it was a deep-seated fear . . .

GINZBURG A deep-seated fear, yes, I had that in the early years of Fascism.

FULVI . . . which you then learned to control.

GINZBURG Which I pushed to one side, yes.

SINIBALDI It reappeared when your father and brother ended up in prison.

5

GINZBURG I was older then, I was seventeen. I remember the first search they did. I remember when they told us that my brother Mario had been caught at the border but had then escaped, that he'd thrown himself into the water, crossed over to Switzerland, and they came in the morning to arrest my father. They had arrested my other brother Gino who was in Ivrea. It was a moment of great . . . a dramatic moment. My mother was there crying; then I remember the people searching the house said if I wanted to go to school, I could, and my mother stuffed into my satchel all her bills [*she laughs*], because she was worried that in all this confusion they would find out that she had these huge bills she owed to a woman who made shirts for her, to her dressmakers . . . so she made me go to school with all these bills in my satchel.

SINIBALDI And this experience of being in prison? For your father, your brother . . .

GINZBURG My father came back. Well, he came back after fifteen or twenty days, rather happy.

FULVI Invigorated by it all, so your stories say.

GINZBURG Yes . . . yes, he was very happy; but in the meantime we had gone through some frightening days, very frightening days. Plus an article had come out that said, "Group of Turin Jews conspire with the anti-Fascists, with Paris exiles," and my mother was terrorized by this word "conspire."

SINIBALDI [*He laughs*] Another of those words that make up the things this family used to say.

FULVI Your mother would soon remember even those incredibly dramatic moments with a certain nostalgia, because tedium was one of her greatest dislikes.

GINZBURG Yes. She would say, "Life has gotten boring again."

SINIBALDI You have spoken of some of the characters, the figures in Turin . . . in the streets, the houses. You've mentioned Pajetta, Vittorio Foa; then there was Salvatorelli,[11] there was the distant figure of Guglielmo Ferrero,[12] there was Cesare Pavese,[13] Leone Ginzburg, Einaudi,[14] Felice Balbo.[15] I'm mixing up different eras.

GINZBURG Yes, different times. I didn't know Pavese then.

SINIBALDI What I meant was that as far as these names are concerned, these names that today are so revered, you depict them with a strange kind of distance . . .

GINZBURG . . . there was Carlo Levi.[16]

SINIBALDI There's a kind of irregularity in the way they are depicted, seen through a child's eyes with detachment, so that some of these characters seem almost squashed, too familiar.

GINZBURG Yes . . . yes, yes.

SINIBALDI . . . whereas others, over time, take on a mythical stature: for example, Rossi[17] and Bauer,[18] who were in prison.

GINZBURG I didn't know Rossi and Bauer but people talked about them. Leone talked about them . . .

SINIBALDI Right, but didn't you also see Leone Ginzburg from this same distance, having heard him being talked about, when he was in prison? Wasn't there in his case, too, this way of looking at him that was a bit—

GINZBURG No, no. Leone Ginzburg I knew before he went to prison, before.

SINIBALDI And then the relationship grew while you were apart?

GINZBURG Well, when he was in prison I would write him letters, because . . . well . . . he was in love with me, and I would write him letters, and he too . . . he would write to his mother and he would send me his love. Then he came out, in '36, and we met up again. He wouldn't come to our house, not then, because at the time you had to be careful, you couldn't be seen together. I would see him outside, we would go for walks and . . . I don't know if my father knew about it at first or not, but he didn't like the idea at all, because—

FULVI Well, he had never approved of anyone.

GINZBURG He had never approved of anyone. But this time he really didn't approve. He said that Leone was ugly, then that he was broke, then that he was in danger. Basically, he didn't like him one bit: well, then at a certain point we got married, and he accepted it. Then afterward he liked him. He would say that Leone was very bright, very well-educated, and later he liked him, but early on there was . . . you know . . . something he didn't like.

SINIBALDI Leone didn't have qualities that brought solidity, perhaps . . .

GINZBURG Right. He had none of those.

SINIBALDI But in reality he was an intellectual of great solidity, of great renown. I'm thinking of that debate on the subject of musical interpretation.[19]

GINZBURG He was one of the real intellects of his time. When I knew him he was twenty-four, so when he was writing for this musical review he was twenty-two. He was exceptional; he always had been. He had an incredibly rich cultural background.

SINIBALDI And did this cultural background influence him a great deal?

GINZBURG Well, he was bilingual.

SINIBALDI Because he was born in Odessa, was from a Russian family, taught Russian literature.

GINZBURG He taught Russian literature. Then he stopped teaching in '33 because he refused to swear an oath of allegiance [to Fascism— *trans.*] . . .

SINIBALDI He was one of the few university professors who refused to swear allegiance.

GINZBURG They had instated the oath for teachers, and so he said he wouldn't do it.

SINIBALDI Then he was one of the founders of the Einaudi publishing house, in a way.

GINZBURG Ah, yes! But not "in a way"! He was very much so. He came back from prison in Civitavecchia in 1936, and Giulio Einaudi went to see him. And they created this publishing house. Which already existed, but they started to do really important books. Then they got in touch with Pavese, and at the start it was those three.

SINIBALDI To go back to the debate on musical interpretation: on that occasion, Leone Ginzburg took a stance that defended an artist's freedom to interpret the text. Was that a small premonition of the stance he took regarding freedom? This legacy of Gobetti,[20] so to speak, which was then handed down to that small group of activists who were a part of Justice and Liberty.

GINZBURG Yes, yes, of course. He was very influenced by Gobetti.

SINIBALDI And was this belief in freedom also common in the anti-Fascist movement, or not? I mean, wasn't it the fundamental belief of both Communists and Socialists?

GINZBURG Yes. Leone wasn't a Communist. He wasn't anti-Communist, but he wasn't a Communist. He wasn't a Zionist, either. There was a group of Jews in Turin who were strong Zionists. He wasn't a Zionist, and I remember he once said, "Zionism is a dangerous thing because it can lead to imperialism." He never thought of Israel as a place where we would go, where we wanted to go. This was very strong in him, that Jews should mix with everyone.

SINIBALDI They should be assimilated, you mean.

GINZBURG Yes.

SINIBALDI As for these figures who were bringing new life to Turin, or beginning to do so . . . they were all very young, as you have pointed out in the case of Leone Ginzburg.

GINZBURG Yes, they were very young. Even Pavese was young.

SINIBALDI Right—even Einaudi was young.

GINZBURG Yes, that's true. In fact, I think that Einaudi was even younger. Leone was born in 1909; Pavese was born in 1909, I think; and Giulio Einaudi in 1912.

SINIBALDI So they were, in effect, just teenagers—it wasn't only Pajetta who was a "red-faced boy." They were all more or less adolescents.

GINZBURG Yes.

SINIBALDI Someone I'd like to call to mind is Carlo Levi.

GINZBURG Well, Carlo Levi was very important in our house. We saw him often. I was seventeen at the time, and I didn't understand that these men were involved in clandestine activity. I understood this when they arrested my brother Mario; but before then, well, I saw them come and go; we would go on Sundays to Barbara Allason's house, where there was a strange succession of people. I remember once Lelio Basso came, and Leone was shut in a room with him, I wondered why on earth—I didn't understand. As for Carlo Levi, I understood later that he was a leader, someone very important. But he was also in my eyes a great painter . . . I thought he was a great painter.

SINIBALDI A friendship that lasted throughout his lifetime, didn't it?

GINZBURG Throughout his lifetime, yes.

SINIBALDI The point you make that he was a key political figure is important here, because Carlo Levi was a great painter, an important and well-known writer after the war, with *Christ Stopped at Eboli*. But his artistic success perhaps eclipsed his importance as an intellectual and a political activist.

GINZBURG Absolutely. But I had found out from Leone that he was an important figure, that he played a key role in their group. Carlo Levi was also arrested when they arrested my brother, but then he was let go. Leone went to prison; he was sent to the special tribunal. Carlo Levi was released, but he was arrested again the following year when there was another wave of arrests. It seems there had been a spy among them, and it turned out to be Pitigrilli. In fact, we know it was Pitigrilli because of letters that have since been found. Vittorio Foa was arrested the next year and was given a stiff sentence. Carlo

Levi was sent into internment, as was my brother Alberto. They were located quite near to one another, and my sister would go and visit them.

SINIBALDI So this familiarity existed. We would like to listen to and let you listen to, now, Carlo Levi's voice. The recording is rather poor quality. It's from 1950 and has been kindly lent to us by the State Record Library.

We are living in times of crisis: and man finds himself faced with forces and institutions that are without limit and beyond his possibilities as an individual. When faced with the mysterious nature of these forces and institutions, his own nature as a man becomes mysterious to him; and the tendency toward a dispersion or breaking up of personality among those huge and faceless institutions is alarmingly powerful. So that every act is a choice, or a defense, or a creation. Faced with the greatness of these forces, which threaten to overwhelm us at all times, every refusal and also every acceptance ask of man a similar greatness, a similar greatness, which, I repeat, requires courage. It is the courage to exist, to be men, not to succumb, when things are at their very worst, to desperation. Not to believe in idols, to resist confusion in the faceless crowd. This courage, this greatness is not only to be found in men who are thinkers, who are powerful, who are involved in the arts. It is not exclusive to writers, painters, architects, musicians, politicians, leaders, scientists, and philosophers—and I shan't give here a list of names that, in any case, would be judged incomplete by those many people, too many, who would claim unjustifiably that they deserved to be featured there—but, perhaps to an even greater extent, it is to be found in all those who have no specific connection to the cultural world but who have nevertheless managed in these last years to preserve man's dignity by making their life, no matter how modest and anonymous, into something with real culture and truly civilized values. It is in these men whose virtue goes unnoticed and not in idolized men that we recognize greatness. We have all witnessed this in years gone by on a daily basis. The Resistance was a moment of popular greatness in which every man, every woman who courageously took part contributed to the salvation of the world's shared patrimony and to that great and mysterious "ideal maturing," in preparation for the future. [21]

And now here is how you once remembered Carlo Levi:

It isn't easy for me to write about Carlo Levi, who was as dear to me as a brother. My memory of him is closely linked to the events, the people, and the years of my youth. The night I found out that he was ill, and was dying, I gathered together inside of me so many scattered memories. I don't think I can talk of him at length as a painter or as a writer or as a political activist. I can only line up my memories.

In recent years I saw him very rarely. When I met him it seemed that I was meeting a crowd of loved and lost beings. This fact, and the great serenity that he exuded, made me feel emotional and happy every time I met him. In fact, I don't know why I didn't try to see more of him. We have, through our youth and the people that were a part of it, ties that are complicated, tortuous, and not easy. They often slow us down. And yet when I met up with Carlo Levi I felt all the tortuousness and complications disappear. and his big, rosy face made me happy. He was someone with whom relationships were direct and light.

The first memories I have of him go back to the time of my adolescence, in Turin, which was his city and mine. He was fourteen years older than me. Fourteen years seemed at the time to be a great deal. He belonged to the adult world, a world to which I yearned to belong with an angst that was like a kind of snobbery, just like someone who wants to climb to a higher and more noble social standing. But I was shy, and this angst stayed hidden. He intimidated me, so much so that in his presence I hardly dared utter a word . . .

He had a large, wide, and rosy face, surrounded by a crown of curls. He used to wear a light-colored coat, almost white in fact; it was a short, wide coat, was always undone and was made from soft, hairy wool. He had corduroy jackets, which at that time nobody was wearing; ornate gold buttons; soft, embroidered ties that were tied in wide knots. He was a friend of my brothers . . . He was a painter, I thought "a great painter," perhaps because it seemed that nothing about him could be mediocre or small, and I never asked myself then or indeed later just how significant his painting was. It seemed to me that in the paintings done by his peers there was squalor and grayness whereas in his there was a joyful riot of color. The landscapes in his paintings seemed beautiful to me, because they were whipped by the wind. It was a wind without dust or gusts, a wind that swept nature along and ruffled it so as to curl it up and make it brighter. The human figures, too, were whipped by the same strong and tempestuous wind that blew at their jackets and ties and blew through their hair, tingeing it with pink, violet, and green hues not so as to offend or mortify these figures, not so as to make them grotesque, but in order to celebrate somehow their arrogance, their complexity, and their glory. Ears and hair that are curled up like this become shells. The world, in his pictures, often seemed to me like a huge beach over which shone a white light where everything was clouds, wind and shells . . .

When I saw him again after a break of many years, in Florence, after the liberation, I no longer felt a great distance between us, partly because I was a lot older and partly because I had seen my share of misfortunes. Besides which he himself seemed to have come down or up from those heights and depths in which I had always seen him. I realized then, during those days in Florence, that in the past he seemed to dwell always either on great mountain heights or in the depths of seas. He had been aloof from and different from people you saw in the street. Now he seemed to be a part of these people. His desire to be different now mingled with a desire to be like other people. . . . Carlo Levi was by nature a person in whom harmony was indestructible and indispensable, just as it is indestructible and indispensable for the sun and for light itself. The world must have seemed to him, in his last years, out of harmony and tiresome, but he loved it all the same and certainly forgave it, out of generosity and goodness and humility; just as, perhaps, he forgave his friends for any indifference and betrayal, which he managed to overlook, gradually, not quickly, as he was incapable of harsh, hasty, or brutal acts.

. . . Last summer he called me and we had dinner together in a trattoria in the center. I hadn't seen him for a while. I didn't find him much older, except that his hair was now completely white, light as feathers, and except for a certain pinkish thinness to his face and neck, which again reminded me of my father. I had always thought there was a vague resemblance in him to my family, perhaps because Jews often have features in common, and his mother had had red hair and there was red hair in my family too, and freckles, and this seemed to establish a kind of kinship between him and us. We were not related, even though my maiden name is the same as his.

That was the last time I saw him . . . We left the restaurant, and I watched him walk one more time into the Rome night, as I had done so many years before, in the time of *Christ Stopped at Eboli*, with his lazy, random, and light-footed step . . . [22]

SINIBALDI I would like to ask Natalia Ginzburg to read a very short extract from *The Things We Used to Say* in which the greatness of Levi is cast in a slightly different light:

My mother started going to the prison with clean clothes again, and she would run into Vittorio's parents there and the relatives of the other detainees. "Such nice people!" she would say of Vittorio's parents. "Such a good family! And they've told me Vittorio is a really fine lad. He's just passed his law exams with flying colors. Alberto has always chosen such respectable friends!"

"And Carlo Levi is inside, too," she would say with a mixture of fear, satisfaction and pride, because it frightened her that so many people had been put inside and that perhaps they were planning a mass trial. But there was also some comfort in the idea that so many were inside, and she was gratified that Alberto was in the company of mature, respectable, and distinguished people. "Professor Guia is inside, too."

"I don't care for Carlo Levi's paintings, though!" my father would retort, since he never missed an opportunity to make it known that he didn't care for Carlo Levi's paintings. "Oh no, Beppino, you're wrong. They're really good," said my mother. "That portrait of his mamma is lovely. You haven't seen it."

"Slathers!" said my father. "I can't abide modern art!"

We might say this is someone looking up from below, don't you think?

GINZBURG Yes.

SINIBALDI . . . which is the kind of dialectic that we are trying to create, juxtaposing various important texts and memories with this familiar tone, which runs through many of the books of Natalia Ginzburg. And now let's talk about literature, let's define Natalia Ginzburg's writing. We decided to call upon an important figure for you to help us at this point: Cesare Garboli, [23] who needs little introduction, being one of the liveliest, most interesting, and sharpest of all Italian critics, borne out in his book *Falbalas*, just published and much reviewed in the papers. He is the official critic of Natalia

13

Ginzburg—if such an honor can exist. It is a form of criticism driven by strong links of—

GINZBURG Friendship.

SINIBALDI Friendship, complicity.

GINZBURG Friendship.

SINIBALDI . . . so plain to see that we don't have to conceal it.

GINZBURG Yes.

SINIBALDI Usually critics and writers hide their friendship, their complicity, because they think it might get in the way of the clarity of the critical vision. It is not so for Garboli. Let's ask Cesare Garboli anyway, who is on the phone now, to help us introduce the writer Natalia Ginzburg. Hello?

CESARE GARBOLI Hello?

SINIBALDI Hello, Cesare Garboli. Natalia Ginzburg is here to say hello and no doubt thanks you for being with us at least telephonically. I say "at least telephonically" because we have not given up hope that for one of these programs you might come to Rome and be with us long enough to talk about your relationship as critic . . . or as "critic-accomplice" of the work of Natalia Ginzburg, who still expresses her gratitude for the advice she gets from Cesare Garboli. Maybe one time she will tell us just what it is, the advice that Garboli has given her over all these years.

GINZBURG Too much to tell. Hello! Hi!

GARBOLI Hi, Natalia! How are you?

GINZBURG I'm fine, fine . . . yes.

GARBOLI And are you still working at the Chamber? What are you doing?

GINZBURG No!? At the Chamber? I'm here! No, Parliament isn't in session!

GARBOLI No, I know that now you're at Rai, but in general, your work at the Chamber still keeps you very busy.

SINIBALDI We've dragged her away from her work at the Chamber to bring her to Rai!

GINZBURG There's been no Chamber for several days because of the elections!

SINIBALDI We have taken advantage of a few days off among MPs. Well, Cesare Garboli . . . obviously there's a lot to say, and we have a lot to ask you. Going back over texts—including the preface to the Meridiani edition of Natalia's works, which is a very illuminating and innovative piece of criticism—I would like you to look back at two things for us. First, your first meeting with Natalia Ginzburg, which, if I am not mistaken, was about a poem that you had read in a Rome review of '44, is that right?

GARBOLI Yes, *Mercurio*.

SINIBALDI That's right, *Mercurio*. So that was the first meeting, but you had already heard of Natalia Ginzburg, is that so?

GARBOLI Yes, I had definitely heard of her, because we had a friend in common . . . a dear person who had been a governess to the Ginzburg family. The father and the mother of Leone Ginzburg were Russian, and they came and spent their holidays in Viareggio. And in Viareggio they had a governess, a helper who was also a friend of my father: Miss Segré. And she introduced Leone Ginzburg to my father. At the time he was just a boy, mind you, just fourteen or fifteen. So, as a child I had heard a lot about Leone and then about Natalia after she married Leone and . . . and that's how she became a person to me. She was one of those people who, when you are a child or teenager, is talked about in the family . . . they become part of the closeness of family. And one day, I was interested in literature, interested in learning, interested in everything cultural as if it were a kind of food. I remember going 'round Rome—I think it was in '45 or even '44—and I found in this review *Mercurio* a poem dedicated to Leone Ginzburg. It was a poem by Natalia about men who go around Rome, buy the papers, live life to the full; because it was a moment in which things were coming back to life—you can imagine Rome in '44, just after being liberated. Things were just coming back to life, and Natalia wrote this poem of pain and nostalgia, of separation, loss. But it wasn't a poem full of mourning. I was fifteen, and it really struck me, because the poem involved a suffering that was somehow stoical, the suffering of someone who doesn't feel suddenly different about the world, about his needs, or his sense of fraternity with the world because he has suffered a loss. I didn't understand at the time that it was a stoical sentiment—because I was too young to understand—but it was also, somehow, a Jewish sentiment. It was one of the first times that I as a child had the revelation of a sensitivity that was not strictly Catholic.

SINIBALDI So this is another reason that coming into contact with the poetry and then the person of Natalia Ginzburg is important to you. The second thing is you have spoken of two phases in Natalia

Ginzburg's work. You have said that there is a more recent Ginzburg, the one that follows *The Things We Used to Say*, with the features that perhaps we recognize more easily, and then there is a "poor" Ginzburg, the one of the earlier writings, the first novels, the texts we are about to talk about. A more austere way of writing, an impoverished perspective on the things of the world and the things of literature. So, how do we distinguish this early approach? What distinguishes the "poor" Ginzburg?

GARBOLI A kind of bare-bones essentiality. The fact that the eye and the sensitivity of the writer, in this case, of Natalia Ginzburg, turns on that element in life that is most essential, almost petrified, if you like. But it is also a way in which Natalia felt she belonged to a condition of living that was in some way shared by all writers at the time, around '39 and '40. Think of the poetry of Montale,[24] for example.

SINIBALDI Of course.

GARBOLI That poetry was trying to be, and was, "unpolished and essential" like pebbles on a stony stretch of sand. This is the Montale of *Cuttlefish Bones*. Also think of Pavese's *A Mania for Solitude*. This search was in the air . . . no, it wasn't a search, it was a state, a way of being. An essentiality that was in some way opposing the triumphalism, the false richness . . .

SINIBALDI And also the rhetoric, don't you think?

GARBOLI . . . of Italy as it was, with its twentieth-century Fascist, or even surrealist, literature. The stripped down essentiality was a rebellion in which poverty became a style, a left-wing rebellion, if you like. I've mentioned Montale, Pavese. I could also mention [Elio] Vittorini, the Vittorini of *Conversation in Sicily*.[25] It is to this movement, in my opinion, that Natalia Ginzburg belongs, that is, the Natalia Ginzburg of the short novel *The Road to the City*. Ginzburg really *begins* with that novel more than with some early stories that were republished in the Meridiani edition of her work. They are interesting stories, interesting as documents as well, as is the story "Mio marito" (My husband).

SINIBALDI "Mio marito," yes.

GARBOLI Well, these are stories in which Ginzburg makes everything happen. Everything—killings, adultery, deaths. She makes everything happen in a few pages with grand gestures, with a great capacity to move through space. But as a narrator, Ginzburg starts in earnest with *The Road to the City*, which was reviewed when it came out—in 1942, if I remember correctly.

GINZBURG Yes.

GARBOLI It was reviewed by a fine critic, Silvio Benco, who found himself presented with a book that was totally new, by a writer nobody had ever heard of—and he was very astute in identifying Natalia's style. I think he spoke of a "direct" style, and of Ginzburg's "scissor-like pace," a direct pace, that is, inflexible, austere, totally devoid of coquettishness, never distracted, and never diverted, the pace of a soldier used to marching long distances; or the pace of those tribal women you find in Hebrew stories, in the Bible, those women wearing shawls, with children in their arms, who put up their tents (no matter what happens, be it war, famine, ravages) and never lose the sense of walking with their feet firmly on the ground precisely because they are used to long marches, to moving on. They put up their tents, prepare food, give birth, get married. Their husbands die, people around them die, but they go on walking, with their child in their arms, they go on cooking, putting up their tents. Those women called Sara, Rebecca, Rachel, those women called Abigail: well, that's how I see Natalia Ginzburg, and I see her from the time she wrote *The Road to the City*—the title says it clearly enough—I see her with this direct pace, used to long marches.

SINIBALDI Cesare Garboli, we are grateful to you for taking part, and we repeat the invitation, I hope not in vain, to join us in person. I don't know if Natalia wants to say good-bye . . .

GINZBURG Thank you so much, Cesare. Thank you.

GARBOLI 'Bye, Natalia!

GINZBURG 'Bye, Cesare. I'll call you, 'bye!

GARBOLI All the best. 'Bye.

SINIBALDI Good-bye. Well, I have nothing to add to Cesare Garboli's words . . .

GINZBURG No, no.

SINIBALDI Naturally it is a surprising image, and one I'm not sure we've heard before, of the Hebrew woman who keeps on walking; and yet it seems to fit, especially as far as the early Ginzburg writings go. Let's listen now to the portrait that Natalia Ginzburg wrote as an adult of a young writer just starting out. It won't be hard to recognize Natalia:

As a young man, he was gifted with imagination. Little, but some at least. The fact of having so little worried him. Having decided and hoped since childhood to be a writer and a novelist, he found it very odd to have so little imagination. He also felt he had very little power of observation. In the world around him he would find a number of very small details and keep them carefully in his memory, but the whole seemed covered in mist. He was very absentminded. Sometimes he wondered what his qualities as a writer were. He couldn't find any in himself. Sometimes he thought he wrote simply because he had decided to do so a long time ago. Deep in himself there was a dark, swirling tumult, like a hidden river, and he felt his writing must come from these waters. But he couldn't pull it up from them.

His imagination was neither adventurous nor generous. It was dry, meager, and thin. He thought of it as a slender, delicate, precious gift and felt that he was coaxing a few sad, languid flowers from a dry soil, whereas he would have liked an enormous landscape of fields and woods. This way, he felt poor. He felt he had to use what he had parsimoniously. He was at once wary, impetuous and parsimonious; impetuous because he thought that if he failed to hurry, his willpower would fade away as well.

His meanness was not merely parsimony, it was real avarice. He thought of a few things and put them down swiftly and dryly. As he wanted to love what he wrote; he called his avarice sobriety. The determination to ignore his own thoughts or to transform them into something noble, lovable, and flattering was stronger than himself.[26]

SINIBALDI This "Portrait of a Writer" from *Never Must You Ask Me* is in reality a self-portrait. We find in it a very important theme—the relationship between invention and experience, between fantasy and reality, and this sober, almost harsh style, which is so typical of the early books of Natalia Ginzburg and which you define here (with harsh self-scrutiny) as a kind of "meanness." Well, I would like to know this: when you started writing you had great role models—Chekhov, the Russians, the authors you read as an adolescent—the precocious tastes you had as an adolescent. Did you experience this lack of a boundless imagination as a burden, a limitation preventing you from recreating Russia, those scenarios, in your Turin?

GINZBURG Yes, I really hated being in Turin. Instead of the Po I wanted there to be a Russian river—the Don, the Neva, yes—and it seemed to me that my father did a job that the father of a writer shouldn't do: he was a university professor, a biologist. Well, I wanted to have as a father, at that time, either a prince or a peasant, or at least something other than a university professor; and this gave me a very strong inferiority complex. As for this kind of "meanness": I felt it deeply, because I had this sense that I had no "background," so to speak, that my cultural background was not rich enough. I felt as if I had very little, partly through lack of experience. I was young, I hadn't lived a lot. But not only for that reason: I felt like someone who had so little that she had to spend what she did have very parsimoniously, with tight control on the purse strings.

SINIBALDI It didn't occur to you that *anyone* of that age has very little?

GINZBURG I did think that.

SINIBALDI That is, at the age when you started writing, thirteen, fourteen years of age.

GINZBURG I did think that, yes, yes, I did. In fact, I used to think, "When I'm older, I'll have learned, studied many things, I'll have a background." But then I didn't. And once, talking to Carlo Levi, who was painting, he said to me, "Yes, your stories are sweet, but you write by chance, you risk writing by chance; fishing by chance for what you need and not having inside of you a deep awareness." And I then thought that you had to write not by chance, that you had to pull from within things that you had inside. And I kept thinking of those words for a long time after.

SINIBALDI It is an extraordinary observation of Levi's because in effect the problem of the young writer is very often the chance nature . . .

GINZBURG The chance nature, yes.

SINIBALDI The fact that he doesn't draw on stimuli, on other people's writings, on models to imitate.

GINZBURG Yes, which also comes from ignorance, from lack of experience, yes.

SINIBALDI But you made up a system, developed a form of self-discipline. I read that you had a notebook in which you would put your ability for observation to the test . . . another talent, another gift that the writer must have.

GINZBURG Yes, yes. I had a tiny notebook in which I wrote things down. But later, these phrases, which I wrote in my notebook, I noticed that when it came to using them, they had frozen there, and I couldn't use them after all. I remember that Soldati once peeked inside this tiny notebook. And there was written, "I go back to being the little sister." And he said, "What does that mean: "I go back to being the little sister"? And . . . well, I had a story in my mind, but still very vaguely, and I didn't know what to say to him about the phrase "I go back to being the little sister." Soldati read my stories when I was very young—I was seventeen—and he took them away. I didn't know where he was going, on a trip, and then he sent me a telegram. I think it was the first telegram I ever received, and in it was written, "Your lovely stories, including 'September,' well done"—um, "Best wishes." And this telegram made me very happy, and I remember that I had said to him, "Yes, there is a story called 'September,' but it's no good," whereas he thought it worked.

SINIBALDI And that was your first review.

GINZBURG The first review, yes.

SINIBALDI Via telegram, like many reviews. And throughout this period you were thinking a lot about yourself.

GINZBURG A great deal.

SINIBALDI About your activity as a writer. But then as time went on, so you said, this self-observation dwindled. Why's that?

GINZBURG Gosh, I don't know. I don't know. For some years now I haven't had ideas for short stories in my head. Once I did, always. Not now, they've gone. I don't think about it anymore: at a certain point I start writing. Then it's born.

SINIBALDI Later we'll talk about the fact that discovering Natalia Ginzburg's novels means also discovering a writing that in some way happens of its own accord, is that so?

GINZBURG Yes . . . yes.

SINIBALDI And we will see how this is the case with the early novels. But there is another rather strange, rather restless feeling of which you have spoken, one that is hard for us to understand: a sense of guilt—am I right?—that has pushed you both to write and not to write, so you have said. So it was a kind of labyrinthine life condition . . .

GINZBURG Yes. I have had many, many feelings of guilt in my life and continue to have them.

SINIBALDI So not only about writing.

GINZBURG Not only about writing. But with writing I felt guilty because I didn't study, not then. I should have studied, first at school, at high school, then I started university but dropped out. I thought that I should study and instead I wrote. Then when I wasn't writing I had the same guilt feeling because I would say, "I should be writing but I'm not writing anything." And I tossed between these guilty feelings . . .

SINIBALDI And did you resolve them?

GINZBURG No.

SINIBALDI And yet after the early stories, which came out of a lack of experience, which you describe as a lack of background, and therefore, came out of the simple desire to write, almost out of a sense of vocation . . . I think this was the chance element for which Carlo Levi reproached you.

GINZBURG Yes.

SINIBALDI The first novels, which we will talk about presently, come out of an experience of life that was partly tragic. Your early life experiences were very painful.

GINZBURG Well, *The Road to the City* I wrote in '41, I think. It came out in '42. In the autumn of '41, I must have written it and . . . I was in internment. My husband Leone Ginzburg had been sent into internment as soon as war broke out. I followed him, we had two small children: *The Road to the City* is a story that was born after I'd been there about a year. I remember that at a certain point Pavese wrote me a postcard: "Dear Natalia, stop having children and write a book that is better than mine." His was *The Harvesters*. And I . . . I was a bit overwhelmed by the children.

SINIBALDI You didn't stop having children, because the third was born there.

GINZBURG No, but I felt compelled to write, to write something. And, well, the first year was very difficult. But then there was the discovery of this village, which was an extraordinary one. We got to know some extraordinary people. There was this village and the nostalgia I felt for my city, for my mother, my friends—and from this feeling . . . I think that often stories, novels are born out of nostalgia. Nostalgia is a much-maligned word these days. Nobody likes using it, but I believe that there is a lovely side to nostalgia. I felt this for Turin, and yet I had before me this village, which I also loved. And from all this *The Road to the City* was born, which is a made-up novel but with real characters whom I met in the village.

SINIBALDI In the village . . .

GINZBURG Yes. This village had a road. I used to walk along this road with my children. This road was strangely compelling: we had a house that looked out onto this road—it wasn't noisy because it was a road completely without traffic. I had these two tiny children, and at a certain point I found a girl who looked after them for me. I would write from three in the afternoon until seven. And I had those hours, and I wrote *The Road to the City*.

SINIBALDI Another element of this self-construction, this discipline, is coldness. In some way, even in *The Road to the City*, even with a feeling so warm as nostalgia, you felt that to be able to write you had to control yourself.

GINZBURG Be detached, yes. At the time I thought . . .

SINIBALDI Invent a style that cooled it down.

GINZBURG Yes, I would first write a page, then I would cut a load of things. And I would rewrite it short, I thought that I had to write it short.

FULVI Perhaps this is a topic that we will need to touch on again later, but from this very first book the attention given to certain female characters is considerable, important. Were you aware of this?

GINZBURG Yes, yes, because I felt that I was inventing a girl I had seen, but in this girl there was me, too, and hidden autobiographical things: my sister, autobiographical things. They were changed a lot, doctored, completely transformed, but there was always an autobiographical vein running through the writing. And then there was me; I'm a woman but I wanted to write like a man. At the time I wanted very much to write like a man . . . not to be clingy.

FULVI Because it went without saying that the concept of "writing like a woman" brought with it this kind of attribute.

GINZBURG At the time I thought so, I was afraid of being clingy.

FULVI Luckily, you didn't go on thinking that way.

GINZBURG No, I didn't.

SINIBALDI We'll listen now to another extract from *Portrait of a Writer*: this guide to your restless thinking and rethinking about your profession:

Sometimes he told himself the truth, though. He told himself that he disliked his own avarice and felt that he was born to be prodigal. He would have liked to pour out rivers of swirling, tumultuous pages, which, at the same time, were limpid and perfect. Whereas his pages were precise in a fast, tidy, clean, and greedy way. In any case this precision was false, because the world he saw before him in fact seemed veiled in fog. So he was not merely greedy, he was a liar. His greediness came from the fear of revealing his bare, uncultivated, foggy world. Only a few thin rays of light peered into this world of his. He picked and counted its dry flowers. All this was done in a hurry, because he felt guilty; he felt a thief: a very greedy, calculating, nervous thief. In clear-sighted moments he found himself hateful.

Yet he comforted himself with the thought that later on, some time in the future, he would suddenly be gifted with great inventiveness and powers of observation. He would have a great fertile imagination, a wild stretch of woodland, and an abundant harvest of thoughts as well; and then he would use his gifts diligently and generously.

Now, his future is merely a stretch of rough, broken, grassless road. His imagination has vanished. He no longer feels a sense of guilt or urgency. He has grown patient. His time is spent undoing what he has done. He despises himself, but without a sense of guilt: he simply despises himself, he dislikes his patience. His greediness has vanished with his imagination: he has become generous and would give away all he had: but sometimes he wonders if he has anything left to give.

SINIBALDI I would like to talk about the early novels of Natalia Ginzburg and the way in which her creative output is linked to a very intense and also tragic experience, coinciding with the end of the 1930s and the beginning of the 1940s. Reading your books— including *The Things We Used to Say*, which is always in our minds as a source of casual insight into your development and that of your female contemporaries—we have the impression that in those years you went through, as did all young women of the "cultured" Turin, a kind of sudden transformation, a brusque passage from childhood or early adolescence into adulthood. In your case, it came with marrying Leone Ginzburg, having your first child, but also because of such dramatic public events as the race laws and then the war. In your opinion, was this a generational experience? This suddenly becoming an adult, this state of being somewhat unprepared for the responsibility?

GINZBURG Yes, I was totally unprepared. In '38 there had been the race laws. Leone had lost his Italian nationality; he had become a stateless person. Then war broke out. They sent him into internment the following day, in a village near Aquila called Pizzoli. I joined him with the children after he had been there, I think, two months. And we found a house: it was a lovely house, there were three big rooms with frescoed ceilings, but there was an awful kitchen. I hated this kitchen [*she laughs*]: because there was a coal-burning stove and I couldn't light it; and I couldn't get used to it, I just couldn't light it. This kitchen would fill up with smoke. Then you could only buy mutton; there was no veal, you couldn't get it, you could get mutton. I found this mutton revolting and inedible, but you had to cook this mutton. But somebody helped me: there was a hotel in Pizzoli called Hotel Vittoria. The owners were a mother and daughter; then there was a son off to war and another son. And this daughter, this girl at the Hotel Vittoria, helped me enormously; she helped all the internees. In the beginning there were only five or six of us. She would come to my house, and she would light this coal-burning stove for me; and then mutton—when I ate it there at the hotel, it was excellent, she would make us delicious meatballs. Whereas when I cooked it, it was awful. I was helped a lot by this girl, a lot: with the children, with getting to know the village. We would spend the evenings in the kitchen of Hotel Vittoria, which was much more welcoming than ours. We would sit by the fire, we didn't talk politics because it wasn't allowed, she didn't want . . . There was the police headquarters nearby. We didn't talk politics there. But with others, with other people in the village, Leone did talk about politics. There was a man called Vittorio Giorgi, whom I saw again quite recently, who was a Communist, and Leone used to spend a lot of time with him. And we got to know many people in the village who would come to see Leone and get him to write letters for them. Various letters of introduction: he was brilliant at writing these letters, he even wrote letters to cardinals, bishops. He would write: "With my devoted greetings, I kiss your holy ring." I thought he was so good at writing these letters. And so we lived very happily in this village, I must say. The second year was easier because we brought in an economy stove from Lanciano, and then we weren't so cold. The stove heated the place up, it was more efficient, there was a tube that went through all the rooms. And everything was easier. We were happy in this village. I must say those were very happy years.

SINIBALDI You with . . .

GINZBURG My children did very well. I would take them for walks along the roads, and workers in the fields would shout at us because it was too cold. They would say the children were too exposed to the wind, the sun, the cold; but the children were fine. And that's how we went on. Three years went by—we spent three years there. Then the twenty-fifth of July came. Leone went . . . left us.

SINIBALDI You always reduce to an everyday dimension even great historical dramas. Historical dramas that were witnessed and felt. Your book *The Road to the City* was published under a pseudonym, the name Alessandra Tornimparte.

GINZBURG It came out with a pseudonym; yes, they told me to find a pseudonym. We thought it up together, Leone and I: the Tornimparte bit came to me because it is a town, a station, out of which trunks were shipped.

SINIBALDI But why a pseudonym? Can you explain why?

GINZBURG Because there was the racial campaign going on. And this book: well, we were given a leave permit for ten days, and we went to Turin. And I took the manuscript to Pavese, and Pavese said he'd publish it, yes, he liked it, he'd publish it. So then this book came out. It was a wonderful moment for me. Menzio designed the dust jacket, which I thought was beautiful. And then, I opened the journal *Primato* one day and there was a terrible, damning review by Alfonso Gatto, who said that he didn't like the book at all. I felt really awful; but then they sent me a very different review by Silvio Benco, which was very favorable.

SINIBALDI Yes, we will discuss in a moment the reactions to the book, and also the kind of influences that, according to the critics, came across in it. But you mentioned the race laws . . .

GINZBURG At the time they seemed . . .

SINIBALDI At the time they seemed?

GINZBURG They seemed not too dramatic. Well, yes, we were internees, we were civilian war internees without any money. At the beginning we had no money, then Adriano Olivetti helped us. So the second year was better.

SINIBALDI Better. But this is how you came to be aware that you were Jews, isn't it?

GINZBURG Jews, yes. But I felt it quite strongly much later. At that time I didn't feel it intensely. Because at the beginning we were only five or six Italian internees. Then some Poles and some Germans arrived, and they told us about awful experiences they'd had. That brought it home to us, this terrible idea that Jews . . . we had already felt it when the Germans took France. When we thought that we were in Hitler's hands it wasn't as if we were unaware of what the Germans were up to. But when we heard it from the lips of these Poles, some of whom knew about relatives who had been taken away, then I felt it more strongly.

SINIBALDI And this awareness endured over time. I say this because we are living through some terrible days.[27]

GINZBURG Terrible days. Yes, I believe I felt myself to be profoundly Jewish after the extermination.

SINIBALDI And I can imagine your reaction to the horrors that we are forced, even in this day and age, to see, to listen to.

GINZBURG Yes, of course, yes. Absolutely.

SINIBALDI I would like to listen to the very beginning of *The Road to the City*, which is your first novel, but also in some way your first book: in the Meridiani edition of your works, for which you decided the order of the books, you put it before your short stories. So it is a valid place to start in order to get to know your literary output. In a certain way, it is the first page of the long narrative by Natalia Ginzburg:

> Nini was the son of one of my father's cousins, and he had been with us ever since he was a little boy. After the death of his parents he went first to live with his grandfather, but the old man used to beat him with a broomstick, and he was always running away to our house. Finally his grandfather died, too, and he was told he could stay with us always.
>
> There were five of us, not counting Nini. The oldest was my sister, Azalea, who had married and gone to live in the city. I came next, and then my three brothers, Giovanni, Gabriele, and Vittorio. They say that big families are happy, but I could never see anything particularly happy about ours. Azalea had married and gone away when she was seventeen, and my ambition was to do likewise. I was seventeen now myself, but I didn't have any offers. Giovanni and Nini were equally restless; in fact, the two smaller boys were the only ones content to stay where they were.
>
> Our house was red with a pergola in front of it, and we hung our clothes on the banisters because we didn't have enough cupboards. "Shoo, shoo!" my mother would say as she chased the hens out of the kitchen. "Shoo, shoo!" All day long the gramophone played the same record over and over again:
>
> > Velvety hands, your sweet perfu-u-me
> > Seems to pervade this cosy room . . . [28]

I would like to read you a short line from that review by Benco, which you quoted, not because—

GINZBURG Yes; before—

SINIBALDI —not because we quote only from positive reviews; because I looked for the one in *Primato* by Alfonso Gatto but it's unobtainable.

GINZBURG Um, I don't have it anymore. I want to say just one thing: that when I wrote that first page, I had absolutely no idea what would come next [*she laughs*]: It was a leap in the dark.

SINIBALDI It was a book that wrote itself, you said so: "I had the whole story in my head; when I started writing novels, I realized that there was this way in which the text wrote itself."

GINZBURG Yes, that's right. I had nothing in my mind. When I wrote "Nini," "the broom," "his grandfather," I had no idea what would come next. Then I remembered an electrician's house (there, in Pizzoli) where there was a girl and where there were those clothes on the stairs and this record. But I found it afterward; I didn't have it in mind before.

SINIBALDI So it was a continuous accumulation of discoveries, small discoveries?

GINZBURG Yes, and then I slid on. But at the beginning . . .

SINIBALDI But at the base lay something solid: that is, an idea of this city, this village. You had always lived in Turin, which was at the time, if not a metropolis, certainly a highly developed city, an advanced city. And from within a small Turin world with very particular characteristics—a cultured, humane world with features that by now we know all too well—you then come up against . . .

GINZBURG A village.

SINIBALDI Could we call it primitive?

GINZBURG Well, yes, because at the time it was a very poor village, very poor. Now it's become like a small Velletri[29]: the country builders have made their money, they've gotten rich. Now it's so clean, it's a small Velletri.

FULVI Is it easy or difficult to go back?

GINZBURG When I went back it was rather difficult. But I saw these people whom I was fond of. The Hotel Vittoria is gone, but I saw this "donna Rosina" who used to take my children on walks for me, who's a grandmother now. I saw her again; sometimes she calls me. She's a girl . . . [*She laughs*] No, no, she's not a girl anymore! She's a grandmother, a lovely person. She got married and had lots of children.

SINIBALDI And there's the Abruzzi countryside in September; and something you had read: Caldwell's *Tobacco Road*,[30] I think you said.

GINZBURG Yes, very vaguely, yes, I had read *Tobacco Road*.

SINIBALDI But is this short circuit between reading and experience a frequent starting point for your books?

27

GINZBURG At the start it was, yes.

SINIBALDI Then that too disappeared.

GINZBURG Now perhaps I don't have that anymore. But perhaps as a guide, it might even be a book I don't like very much, but which leads me toward writing.

SINIBALDI But the Caldwell we can probably understand: a book about a primitive America.

GINZBURG I read it then, yes. I was incredibly influenced by Pavese, I have to say, in those years.

SINIBALDI And therefore also by books that Pavese suggested you read.

GINZBURG Yes, but also by Pavese's writing.

SINIBALDI And similarities to *The Harvesters* have been found in *The Road to the City*.

GINZBURG Well, I had *The Harvesters* in my head at the time.

SINIBALDI So for once the critics didn't get it wrong.

GINZBURG No, no, no.

SINIBALDI Let's bring in Benco, the one who picked up straightaway on some of the qualities of Natalia Ginzburg. A very sensitive critic. He wrote, for example, "Her style, with its short phrases, is always as it should be: quick, direct, even, with nothing exclamatory, it walks along like life itself." Garboli, I remember, agreed with this kind of image. And then Benco made a prophecy: "There is no need for her, Natalia Ginzburg, to use words that are not inherent in the story. The author truly loves the throbbing pulse of what is real; I don't think she will ever launch herself into the building of a fantasy world."[31] Is there truth in this?

GINZBURG Yes, those words helped me a lot.

SINIBALDI I imagine they were gratifying to hear.

GINZBURG Very.

SINIBALDI But did the prophecy fulfill itself? I mean, have you never launched yourself into the building of a fantasy world?

GINZBURG No, never. "A fantasy world": I think he meant surrealism in some way.

SINIBALDI Pure invention, fantasy, the fantastic.

GINZBURG No, no, never. I never had these temptations. I think that both damning and positive critiques are useful.

SINIBALDI But the positive ones are more so. [*He laughs*]

GINZBURG Yes, but a good beating also, the good beating that Alfonso Gatto gave me, I think it was useful.

SINIBALDI Well, let's not forget Levi's harsh attack when he accused you of writing by chance, which is a pretty radical criticism, I think, behind the affection. This is the first book written not by chance, isn't it?

GINZBURG Yes.

SINIBALDI In *The Road to the City* there are some fairly typical figures. There's this apathetic married couple; there are these weak, inept male figures. Did these derive from experience or intuition?

GINZBURG Gosh, I don't know. I couldn't say. I was surrounded by men who weren't like that, not at all.

SINIBALDI Energetic, intelligent men.

GINZBURG My brothers and Leone. No, they weren't like that. I don't know why: well, there was in the story this figure of Nini who was lazy, but he was—

SINIBALDI Rich, he had his own richness.

GINZBURG —rich, with a poetic life in his soul, which [the female character—*trans.*] doesn't reach. Who knows? I don't know . . .

SINIBALDI There's another unique aspect, a phrase that comes up every now and again in the book, a kind of curse: "Damn the mother who made you!" Why? Given the theme of motherhood—you, in spite of everything—how can I say it? Isn't it a bit surprising?

GINZBURG No, no.

SINIBALDI In spite of the hard times, really hard, you decided to have two, three children, something we can now interpret, with hindsight, as an act of faith in life. Well, people have children for many different reasons: but if we think of a young woman sent into internment with a man being persecuted for his political beliefs whose future is uncertain, with the added burden of the race laws, then to have children, it seems like an act of optimism.

GINZBURG Of trust.

SINIBALDI Of trust in life—now I don't want to enquire if—

GINZBURG Well, "Damn the mother who made you!" was a phrase, you see, that they used in Pizzoli, a lot.

SINIBALDI And it seemed to strike a chord.

GINZBURG Yes. "Damn the mother who made you!"—I didn't think about it from an ideological point of view, I saw it as a way . . . as a set phrase.

SINIBALDI But one of profound despair because it is the denial of the right to be born, isn't it?

GINZBURG Yes, but I don't think it came across like that here.

SINIBALDI [*He laughs*] No, I suppose not, of course.

GINZBURG It was a phrase that came up often, yes.

SINIBALDI You have already mentioned that very few political discussions went on during internment, so how did you follow events, politics? Was there some kind of exchange under the pretext of the work going on at Einaudi?

GINZBURG Yes, Leone started working again for Einaudi at a certain point.

SINIBALDI And this was also a channel of political communication.

GINZBURG Yes, of course. But we did talk politics a little with the other internees. We didn't talk about it in the kitchen of Hotel Vittoria, because we couldn't, because they would have thought it dangerous. You see, the village had taken us into their hearts, but I don't think they thought we were anti-Fascists. They thought we were Jews. They didn't ask questions. Leone talked politics with Vittorio Giorgi, who was a Communist; then with the ironmonger, someone called Attilio. With the others, with the villagers, we talked about the war: we would say, "Let's hope the war ends soon." "When are you going home?" they would ask us. "When do you go back to your own homes?" They would say that all the time.

SINIBALDI But was there not even something organized by an underground political organization?

GINZBURG In the village?

SINIBALDI In which Leone Ginzburg was involved. Was there nothing?

GINZBURG Not at that time. He had been involved before.

SINIBALDI Yes, of course, and would be again later.

GINZBURG But during internment, no, it wasn't possible. All our letters were read, and Leone had to go every day and report to the local police at ten in the morning.

SINIBALDI So this cut off all possibilities. We've said already how nevertheless this period was to become one that you remember with nostalgia, because it represents a kind of happy interval before what would happen next.

GINZBURG Yes, well, after the eighth of September I was on my own.

SINIBALDI Everything would change, end. There's a text you wrote in Rome in '44 called "Winter in the Abruzzi." Leone Ginzburg had died, everything had changed, and we can really sense the nostalgia and also the happiness that you attributed to this period spent in the Abruzzi. We'll hear it now. It has been republished in *The Little Virtues*, but at the time it came out in *Aretusa*, I think.

GINZBURG In *Aretusa*.

SINIBALDI Which was one of the livelier of the reviews that did so well after the war.

GINZBURG Yes, I had written *Deus nobis haec otia fecit* (God has given us this moment of peace), by which I meant that we had been so happy there.

SINIBALDI Let's listen now to "Winter in the Abruzzi."

God has given us this moment of peace

There are only two seasons in the Abruzzi: summer and winter. The spring is snowy and windy like the winter, and the autumn is hot and clear like the summer. Summer starts in June and ends in November. The long days of sunshine on the low, parched hills, the yellow dust in the streets and the babies' dysentery come to an end, and winter begins. People stop living in the streets: the barefoot children disappear from the church steps. In the region I am talking about almost all the men disappeared after the last crops were brought in: they went for work to Terni, Sulmona, or Rome. Many bricklayers came from that area, and some of the houses were elegantly built; they were like small villas with terraces and little columns, and when you entered them you would be astonished to find large dark kitchens with hams hanging from the ceilings, and vast, dirty, empty rooms. In the kitchen a fire would be burning, and there were various kinds of fire: there were great fires of oak logs, fires of branches and leaves, fires of twigs picked up one by one in the street. It was easier to tell the rich from the poor by looking at the fires they burnt than by looking at the houses or at the people themselves, or at their clothes and shoes, which were all more or less the same.

When I first arrived in that countryside all the faces looked the same to me; all the women—rich and poor, young and old—resembled one another. Almost all of them had toothless mouths: exhaustion and a wretched diet, the unremitting overwork of childbirth and breast-feeding mean that women lose their teeth there when they are thirty. But then, gradually, I began to distinguish Vincenzina from Secondina, Annunziata from Addolerata, and I began to go into their houses and warm myself at their various fires.

When the first snows began to fall a quiet sadness took hold of us. We were in exile: our city was a long way off, and so were books, friends, the various desultory events of a real existence. We lit our green stove with its long chimney that went through the ceiling: we gathered together in the room with the stove—there we cooked and ate, my husband wrote at the big oval table, the children covered the floor with toys. There was an eagle painted on the ceiling of the room, and I used to look at the eagle and think that was exile. Exile was the eagle, the murmur of the green stove, the vast, silent countryside, and the motionless snow. At five o'clock the bell of the Church of Santa Maria would ring and the women with their black shawls and red faces went to Benediction. Every evening my husband and I went for a walk: every evening we walked arm in arm, sinking our feet into the snow. The houses that ran alongside the street were inhabited by people we knew and liked, and they all used to come to the door to greet us. Sometimes one would ask, "When will you go back to your own house?" My husband answered, "When the war is over." "And when will this war be over? You know everything and you're a professor, when will it be over?" They called my husband "the professor" because they could not pronounce his name, and they came from a long way off to ask his advice on the most diverse things—the best season for having teeth out, the subsidies which the town-hall gave and the different taxes and duties.

In winter when an old person died of pneumonia the bell of Santa Maria sounded the death knell, and Domenico Orecchia, the joiner, made the coffin. A woman went mad, and they took her to the lunatic asylum at Collemaggio, and this was the talk of the countryside for a while. She was a young, clean woman, the cleanest in the whole district; they said it was excessive cleanliness that had done it to her. Girl twins were born to Gigetto di Calcedonio who already had twin boys, and there was a row at the town hall because the authorities did not want to give the family any help as they had quite a bit of land and an immense kitchen garden. A neighbor spat in the eye of Rosa, the school caretaker, and she went about with her eye bandaged because she intended to pay back the insult. "The eye is a delicate thing, and spit is salty," she explained. And this was talked about for a while until there was nothing else to say about it.

Every day homesickness grew in us. Sometimes it was even pleasant, like being in gentle, slightly intoxicating company. Letters used to arrive from our city with news of marriages and deaths from which we were excluded. Sometimes our homesickness was sharp and bitter and turned into hatred; then we hated Domenico Orecchia, Gigetto di Calcedonio, Annunziatina, the bells of Santa Maria. But it was a hatred that we kept hidden because we knew it was unjust; and our house was always full of people who came to ask for favors and to offer them. Sometimes the dressmaker made a special kind of dumpling for us. She would wrap a cloth round her waist and beat the eggs, and send Crocetta around the countryside to see if she could borrow a really big saucepan. Her red face was absorbed in her work, and her eyes shone with a proud determination. She would have burnt the house down to make her dumplings come out a success. Her clothes and hair became white with flour and then she would place the dumplings with great care on the oval table where my husband wrote.

Crocetta was our serving woman. In fact, she was not a woman since she was only fourteen years old. It was the dressmaker who had found her. The dressmaker divided the world into two groups—those who comb their hair and those who do not comb their hair. It was necessary to be on the lookout against those who do not comb their hair because, naturally, they have lice. Crocetta combed her hair; and so she came to work for us and to tell our children tall tales about death and cemeteries. Once upon a time there was a little boy whose mother died. His father chose another wife, and this stepmother didn't love the boy. So she killed him when his father was out in the fields, and she boiled him in a stew. His father came home for supper, but, after he had finished eating, the bones that were left on the plate started to sing.

> Mummy with an angry frown
> Popped me in the cooking pot,
> When I was done and piping hot
> Greedy daddy gulped me down.

Then the father killed his wife with a scythe, and he hung her from a nail in front of the door. Sometimes I find myself murmuring the words of the song in the story, and then the whole country is in front of me again, together with the particular atmosphere of its seasons, its yellow gusting wind and the sound of its bells.

Every morning I went out with my children, and there was a general amazed disapproval that I should expose them to the cold and the snow. "What sin have the poor creatures committed?" people said. "This isn't the time for walking, dear. Go back home."

I went for long walks in the white deserted countryside, and the few people I met looked at the children with pity. "What sin have they committed?" they said to me. There, if a baby is born in the winter they do not take it out of the room until the summer comes. At midday my husband used to catch up with me at the post office and we went back to the house together.

I talked to the children about our city. They had been very small when we left and had no memories of it at all. I told them that there the houses had many stories, that there were so many houses and so many streets and so many big fine shops. "But here there is Giro's," the children said.

Giro's shop was exactly opposite our house. Giro used to stand in the doorway like an old owl, gazing at the street with his round, indifferent eyes. He sold a bit of everything: groceries and candles, postcards, shoes and oranges. When the stock arrived and Giro unloaded the crates, boys ran to eat the rotten oranges that he threw away. At Christmas, nougat, liqueurs, and sweets also arrived. But he never gave the slightest discount on his prices. "How mean you are, Giro," the women said to him, and he answered "People who aren't mean get eaten by dogs." At Christmas the men returned from Terni, Sulmona and Rome, stayed for a few days, and set off again after they had slaughtered the pigs. For a few days people ate nothing but "sfrizzoli," incredible sausages that made you drink the whole time; and then the squeal of the new piglets would fill the street.

In February the air was soft and damp. Gray, swollen clouds traveled across the sky. One year during the thaw the gutters broke. Then water began to pour into the house, and the rooms became a veritable quagmire. But it was like this throughout the whole area, not one house remained dry. The women emptied buckets out of their windows and swept water out of their front doors. There were people who went to bed with an open umbrella. Domenico Orecchia said that it was punishment for some sin. This lasted for a week; then, at last, every trace of snow disappeared from the roofs, and Aristide mended the gutters.

A restlessness awoke in us as winter drew to its end. Perhaps someone would come to find us: perhaps something would finally happen. Our exile had to have an end, too. The roads that separated us from the world seemed shorter; the post arrived more often. All our chilblains gradually got better.

There is a kind of uniform monotony in the fate of man. Our lives unfold according to ancient, unchangeable laws, according to an invariable and ancient rhythm. Our dreams are never realized, and as soon as we see them betrayed we realize that the most intense joys of our life have nothing to do with reality. No sooner do we see them betrayed than we are consumed with regret for the time when they glowed within us. And in this succession of hopes and regrets our life slips by.

My husband died in Rome, in the prison of Regina Coeli, a few months after we left the Abruzzi. Faced with the horror of his solitary death and faced with the anguish that preceded his death, I ask myself if this happened to us—to us, who bought oranges at Giro's and went for walks in the snow. At that time I believed in a simple and happy future, rich with hopes that were fulfilled, with experiences and plans that were shared. But that was the best time of my life, and only now that it has gone from me forever—only now do I realize it.[32]

SINIBALDI In "Winter in the Abruzzi," we are presented with the theme of memory. A painful motif in this case but one that will be precious in helping us understand the narrative of Natalia Ginzburg. And "Winter in the Abruzzi" closes with the laconic allusion to the death of Leone Ginzburg. We don't want to add much to this, and besides we will talk more about Leone Ginzburg again. Let us leave his death with that brief allusion, to which we add a well-known text: the letter Leone sent Natalia from prison, which is included in the volume *Lettere di condannati a morte della Resistenza italiana* (Letters by condemned men of the Italian Resistance):

Dear Natalia, my love,

Every time I hope that this letter I am writing will not be the last, before leaving or in general; and that is how it is today as well. I am still feeling, almost a whole day later, the happy excitement that your news brought me and the tangible proof that you love me so. This excitement could not be cancelled out either by the unexpected encounter we had today. Things, it must be said, do not augur well; but let's not worry. All the same, should they make me leave, do not follow me under any circumstances. You are much more necessary to the children, and especially to the little one.

And I would never have any peace if I knew you were exposed for who knows how long to dangers, which should end soon for you and not keep growing greater by the day. I know of how much comfort I am depriving myself by doing this; but it would be a comfort poisoned with fears for you and remorse for the children. Besides, we must not give up hope of seeing each other again sooner or later, and so many emotions will form and fade in our memory until it becomes something that is bearable and coherent. But let's talk of something else. One of the things that most upsets me is the ease with which those around me (and sometimes I as well), when faced with personal danger, lose all interest in problems in general. So I shall try not to talk about me, but about you. What I wish for is that you bring some normality, as soon as you are able, to your existence; that you work and write and are useful to others. This advice will seem facile and irritating; but in fact it is the best that my fondness for you and my sense of responsibility can offer. Through artistic creation you will be liberated from the tears that well up inside you and threaten to overwhelm you; by mixing socially, no matter in what way, you will stay close to the world of others, a world to which I was so often your only means of access. Anyway, having the children will mean for you having a great resource of strength to draw on. I would like Andrea, too, to remember me, even if he never got to see me again. I think of them all the time, but I try not to dwell on these thoughts or else I would sink into gloom. Whereas the thought of you I don't chase away, and it almost always makes me stronger. Seeing friendly faces these last few days left me so excited, as you can imagine. Now my life is getting back to normal again, before it changes more radically. I must stop because I've started writing too late; trusting in the light from my little lamp, which is unfortunately particularly faint tonight as well as being so high up. I will carry on writing without seeing and without any hope of being able to reread it. The fact that I am in the midst of reading Tommaseo at the moment makes me see a similarity between this and a page of his diary written when his sight was failing. I, fortunately, am blind only until tomorrow morning. 'Bye, my love, my tender love. In a few days it will be our sixth wedding anniversary. How and where will I be on that day? What mood will you be in? I have been thinking, just recently, about our life together. Our only enemy (I concluded) was my fear. The times when I, for some reason, was beset with fear and would focus so much of my attention on overcoming it and on not letting people down that there was no other kind of life left in me. Isn't that so? If and when we will be together again, I will be free from fear, and not even these opaque zones will exist any longer in our life together. How much I love you, dear Natalia. If I ever lost you, I would willingly die. (This is another of the conclusions I have reached just recently.)

But I don't want to lose you, and I don't want you to lose yourself even if, by some chance, it is I who am lost. Say hello from me, and thank everyone who is good and affectionate with you: there must be many of them. Ask your mother, ask all your family, to forgive all the trouble that this all-too-numerous family of ours brings. Give the children a kiss from me. I bless all four of you and thank you for being in the world. I love you, I kiss you, my love. I love you with every fiber of my being. Don't worry on my account. Imagine I am a prisoner of war; there are so many of them, especially in this war, and the large majority will return. We can hope to be in this majority, can't we, Natalia?

I kiss you again and again and again. Be brave.

Leone

37

SINIBALDI I don't think that requires any comment. I would like to read a poem called *Memory*, which Garboli mentioned earlier. He said that it marked his first encounter with the writings of Natalia Ginzburg.

Memory

Men come and go through the city's streets.
They buy food and newspapers, they have their jobs to do.
They have rosy faces, rich, full lips.
You lifted the sheet to look at his face,
You leaned down to kiss him in the same old way.
But it was the last time. It was the same face,
Just a little more tired. And the suit was the same.
And the shoes were the same. And the hands were those
That would break the bread and pour the wine.
Today, with time moved on, you still lift the sheet
To see his face for the last time.
If you walk along the street, nobody is beside you.
If you are afraid, nobody takes your hand.

And it isn't your street, it isn't your city.
It isn't your city which is all lit up: the city all lit up belongs to
    others,
To the men who come and go buying food and newspapers.
You can look out for a while from the quiet window
And look in silence at the garden in the dark.
Then when you cried there was his calming voice.
Then when you laughed there was his obliging smile.
But the gate that would be opened at night will be shut forever;
And your youth is gone, the fire is out, the house is empty.

TWO

WORKING LIFE

MARINO SINIBALDI In 1945, with the war over, Natalia Ginzburg settles first in Rome, then in Turin, and starts working for Einaudi. Life goes on, picks up where it left off, with the friends and acquaintances in Turin.

NATALIA GINZBURG Of course.

SINIBALDI This was a very important decision for you.

GINZBURG Yes, yes, of course.

SINIBALDI To be on your own in Rome.

GINZBURG Yes, of course. I wanted to earn money. I wanted to work and earn money, because I had these children to support. So I went to the Einaudi publishing house to see Muscetta.

SINIBALDI In Rome, that is.

GINZBURG Muscetta was in Rome, yes. I came down to Rome from Florence, and I went to see Muscetta and I asked him if he'd take me on, and he did. And I started working there. At first I thought he didn't really know what I should do. But then he handed me a manuscript, *The Story of Gösta Berling*, to read through, and I worked on this translation of *Gösta Berling*. It was my first job. Then he gave me a translation to work on of Mérimée's *Carmen* by Sandro Penna, and I worked on that. Then I translated *The Silence of the Sea* by Vercors, and then—

SINIBALDI Then you started your translation of Proust.

GINZBURG Yes, then I started working again on my translation of Proust.

SINIBALDI And in Turin, how . . . ?

GINZBURG They were transferring the publishing house, they were closing the Rome office. Pavese stayed behind, he stayed for a while longer, and I went to Turin. In the early days it was me and Mila, I worked in a room with Mila. And then Felice Balbo came from Rome, and then Pavese.

SINIBALDI How did you find that small world that you had known before the war, in both Rome and Turin? Did you find the people, relationships had changed? Had the Resistance united or actually divided people?

GINZBURG Well, no, it had united them. There was a sense of union, of solidarity, at the beginning. There was a sense of profound friendship between people, which had started during the Resistance and was ongoing. At the Einaudi publishing house there was a very strong sense that things were starting up again. It was wonderful. Everyone was very close, we were always talking about things, driven by a desire to get on with it.

SINIBALDI And by enthusiasm. And yet the text that you wrote and published in Turin in '46 called "The Son of Man."

GINZBURG Yes.

SINIBALDI . . . is more of a bemused response, daunted even, to what had gone on. Faced with the widespread will to heal, you were saying—we'll hear it in a moment—"You can't heal from what has happened." Was this your attitude?

GINZBURG Yes . . . well, yes, we also had this overwhelming feeling, of cities destroyed, the bombing that had torn the insides out of houses.

SINIBALDI A wound that could not heal over.

GINZBURG Something that could not heal over, yes.

SINIBALDI Well, let's listen to "The Son of Man":

We shall not get over this war. It is useless to try. We shall never be people who go peacefully about their business, who think and study and manage their lives quietly. Something has happened to our houses. Something has happened to us. We shall never be at peace again.

We have seen reality's darkest face, and it no longer horrifies us. And there are still those who complain that writers use bitter, violent language, that they write about cruel, distressing things, that they present reality in the worst possible light.

We cannot lie in our books, and we cannot lie in any of the things we do. And perhaps this is the one good thing that has come out of the war. Not to lie, and not to allow others to lie to us. Such is the nature of the young now, of our generation. Those who are older are still too fond of falsehoods, of the veils and masks with which they hide reality. Our language saddens and offends them. They do not understand our attitude to reality. We are close to the truth of things. This is the only good the war has given us, but it has given it only to the young. It has given nothing but fear and a sense of insecurity to the old. And we who are young are also afraid, we also feel insecure in our homes, but we are not rendered defenseless by this fear. We have a toughness and strength that those who are older than us have never known.

For some the war started only with the war, with houses reduced to rubble and with the Germans, but for others it started as long ago as the first years of Fascism, and consequently for them the feeling of insecurity and constant danger is far greater. Danger, the feeling that you must hide, the feeling that without warning you will have to leave the warmth of your bed and your house— for many of us all this started many years ago. It crept into our childish games, followed us to our desks at school and taught us to see enemies everywhere. This is how it was for many of us in Italy and elsewhere, and we believed that one day we would be able to walk without anxiety down the streets of our own cities, but now that we can perhaps walk there without anxiety we realize that we shall never be cured of this sickness. And so we are constantly forced to seek out a new strength, a new toughness with which to face whatever reality may confront us. We have been driven to look for an inward peace, which is not the product of carpets and little vases of flowers.

There is no peace for the son of man. The foxes and the wolves have their holes, but the son of man hath nowhere to lay his head. Our generation is a generation of men. It is not a generation of foxes and wolves. Each of us would dearly like to rest his head somewhere, to have a little warm, dry nest. But there is no peace for the son of man. Each of us at some time in his life has had the illusion that he could sleep somewhere safely, that he could take possession of some certainty, some faith, and there rest his limbs. But all the certainties of the past have been snatched away from us, and faith has never after all been a place for sleeping.

And we are people without tears. The things that moved our parents do not move us at all. Our parents and those older than us disapprove of the way we bring up our children. They would like us to lie to our children as they lied to us. They would like our children to play with woolly toys in pretty pink rooms with little trees and rabbits painted on the walls. They would like us to surround their infancy with veils and lies, to carefully hide the truth of things from them. But we cannot do this. We cannot do this to children whom we have woken in the middle of the night and tremblingly dressed in the darkness so that we could flee with them or hide them or simply because the air raid sirens were lacerating the skies. We cannot do this to children who have seen terror and horror in our faces. We cannot bring ourselves to tell these children that we found them under cabbages or that when a person dies he goes on a long journey.

There is an unbridgeable abyss between us and the previous generation. The dangers they lived through were trivial, and their houses were rarely reduced to rubble. Earthquakes and fires were not phenomena that happened constantly and to everyone. The women did their knitting and told the cook to make for lunch and invited their friends to houses that did not collapse. Everyone thought and studied and managed his life quietly. It was a different time and probably very fine in its way. But we are tied to our suffering, and at heart we are glad of our destiny as men.[1]

SINIBALDI That is how you described the abyss that had formed between the before and the after. Nobody was as they had been.

GINZBURG Yes, of course.

SINIBALDI That is, everything became an adventure, and difficult. Your flight from internment, for example. Everything was so hard, so new: but then also new to you were the forms of solidarity, which perhaps had not been so common in the small world of Turin in which you had grown up, they didn't have this importance.

GINZBURG Yes, of course. But the last days as an internee were frightening for me, because really, when the Germans got there, we were afraid. All the internees were afraid, especially the German Jews. They were terrified. So we lived moments of sheer terror: this village, which had seemed so peaceful, so quiet, suddenly frightened me. Then I got a letter from Leone telling me to leave immediately. In Rome on the sixteenth of October they had deported the Jews. He was in Rome, working underground. He told me to get away any way I could. But I didn't know how; so the people in the village helped me. The girl from the Hotel Vittoria helped me, and that Communist, Vittorio Giorgi, those two: they all met up that day at my house. They said, "This is about saving a family," and [she cries] . . . and this girl went to the German soldiers who were staying in her hotel and she said to them that she had a cousin who had been evacuated from Naples who had lost her papers in the bombings, and asked them if they could take us to Rome in their lorry. And we left on a German lorry with the village waving us off.

SINIBALDI I don't know if it is as a consequence of this discovery of the world . . . of the simple world, that your relationship with politics became a lot closer after the war. Before, you were more of a spectator. Turati hid in his parents' house during his escape from Italy, that famous escape organized by Rosselli, Parri, Pertini, and Adriano Olivetti. The way history, groundbreaking politics, had descended, almost fleetingly, onto your house, it had left you . . . unchanged. You were a girl, a little girl who simply stood by and watched, with excitement and perhaps the tiniest bit of fear, as these great moments in history glided through the walls and corridors of your home.

GINZBURG Well, after my brother's arrest . . . he had been caught at Ponte Tresa and threw himself into the water and fled to Switzerland. Leone had been arrested; so, there had been . . .

SINIBALDI There was that series of roundups against the JL groups, the Justice and Liberty groups, which included all your friends.

GINZBURG Yes, that was a very dramatic time. And then there was the racial campaign, internment. And during internment, times were peaceful for us, but we were thinking of all the things we would do. I was thinking I would do things.

SINIBALDI Political things? So you were beginning to think of your future political activity?

GINZBURG Yes political . . . political.

SINIBALDI So how did you make the leap, decide to get into politics? It was only really after the war, wasn't it?

GINZBURG Yes, right after the war I joined Partito d'Azione.[2] I was a member of Partito d'Azione. Then I went up to Turin from Rome, and in Turin I became a Communist. In the meantime Partito d'Azione—

SINIBALDI —was disbanded.

GINZBURG It disbanded, and I thought I wanted to be a Communist. And Balbo took me.

SINIBALDI Here is a key figure among the ones you've called to mind.

GINZBURG Yes, he was an important figure, very important.

SINIBALDI This Felice Balbo[3] : an important figure for you and also one of the hardest to place, perhaps.

GINZBURG Well, because he was different, very different from the rest. But there was a strong bond between him; Pavese; Calvino, who at a certain point joined the publishing house, I think in '47, and . . . well, then we were Communists. We were Communists also because we had this memory of Russia fighting against Hitler; yes, we had this memory above all.

SINIBALDI This was the main reason?

GINZBURG Well, the idea that above all we must fight Nazism in whatever form it might come back.

SINIBALDI And wasn't there also the awareness . . . I mean, I imagine that the people of Pizzoli, the people as a whole, were Communist.

GINZBURG Yes, of course, the desire to get out of our privileged social classes and to be united, there was that.

SINIBALDI A move toward the people, then.

GINZBURG Yes, there was that. It was very difficult because we all felt, at least I felt a lot, the desire for creative freedom, and Communism frightened me, but . . .

SINIBALDI But it seemed secondary at the time?

GINZBURG It seemed secondary at the time. It seemed that later freedom would be achieved.

SINIBALDI So when did you realize that it was not secondary? You left the Communist Party at the beginning of the fifties.

GINZBURG Years after . . . well, I followed Balbo. When Balbo left, I left, too.

SINIBALDI So, let's remember Felice Balbo, because he is, I repeat, an extremely important figure for you, extremely important in the development of the Einaudi publishing house, and yet he is unfairly placed in the second tier compared—

GINZBURG That's true, yes, that's true.

SINIBALDI Perhaps because he didn't have a creative outlet or one that made its mark through the writing of books.

GINZBURG Well, he wrote; later on Boringhieri published his works.

SINIBALDI But his work seems also to be that of a great reader, a great analyzer, a careful listener to whatever was going on.

GINZBURG Yes, an extremely careful listener.

SINIBALDI Many years later, in 1970, you remembered this former friend of yours, Felice Balbo, and his influence in those years, in a text that came out in *La Stampa* and was then published in *Never Must You Ask Me*. As often happens in your work, the starting point for the text is a small event, a tiny episode—I think it was something personal, an offer of work—which then ends up offering a kind of judgment on politics. The text we are going to hear now is called "Two Communists":

Some time around last Christmas a man rang me up. He said he wanted to suggest some work for me. He came; I had never seen him before and I liked him very much. We talked for a long time about a number of things. I know and can say nothing about him except that he was very likeable and that he worked for television. He asked me if I would make an enquiry on women in Italy, for television. I said I didn't know how to make enquiries and didn't at all like thinking "about women," that is, about women's problems separated from those of men. I told him that I didn't like traveling, either. I shouldn't in the least like traveling around Italy with cameramen. I told him that the only thing in the world I loved was writing whatever came into my head. He told me I wouldn't have to travel because other people would do the traveling for me. I could stop at home. And he said that I wouldn't be doing the work alone because a sociologist would be working with me. The idea of working with a sociologist terrified me, and I refused. I felt I shouldn't be able to talk to a sociologist: that sociology was too distant from me. Then he told me the name of the sociologist they had thought of writing to, to see whether he would agree. It was Ardigò. I don't know him well, but I have known him for years. I think well of him, I like him. We have in common the memory of a friend. This friend was Felice Balbo, who died in 1964. Suddenly I wanted to see Ardigò, whom I never see. Felice Balbo had a great many friends, people quite different from one another who had nothing in common but the habit of arguing with him late into the night. As a rule these discussions took place standing up, because he used to stand, and the talk became particularly heated on the landing, just as one was saying good-bye. I thought that

47

Balbo might have been pleased if Ardigò and I, his two friends, worked together in an enquiry on women in Italy.

When he left, this pleasant man told me that he would let me know if Ardigò accepted. It didn't strike me, until he had gone, that until then I'd never realized that Ardigò was a sociologist. In fact, I'd never wondered what he was. To me he was a friend of Balbo's, and that was enough. I didn't like all Balbo's friends, but I liked Ardigò. My liking of him was based on impressions that were fleeting but quite precise. I made a list of the things I knew about him. He was pleasant. He lived in Bologna. He had a blonde sister whom I had met in the mountains. I thought how rough, limited, and confused my ideas about people often were. And I thought that this limitation of mine, this poverty of ideas in myself, gave me a feeling of melancholy, poverty, and confusion. I felt, somehow, that I was moving in empty space. I thought that I was the last person in the world who could make an enquiry with a sociologist. As I so often moved in mist and emptiness, I couldn't talk to politicians or sociologists, people who must turn lucid, precise, and factual eyes on reality. I thought that Ardigò would despise me at once. Or that something even worse might happen, that is, he might be mistaken and think I had a culture and a social penetration I hadn't really got at all. I thought how hard it was to be understood. Being understood means being taken and accepted for what we are. The saddest danger we run with other people is not so much that they don't see or don't love our qualities, but that they suppose these real qualities of ours have given birth to all kinds of other qualities that, in fact, are completely nonexistent. And I thought that Felice Balbo's best quality, in relation to other people, was that he was never wrong about them, never gave them gifts they didn't possess. Instead, he tried to bring out the most vital, the most profound and central part of anyone he was with, he tried to choose and to liberate the best the other person had in him, and that alone, without a trace of surprise, scorn, or mockery at the other person's limitations or poverty. In fact, when he was with someone else, he spent his time in the only place where the other's intelligence could follow him unrestrictedly. When he was with others, he never sought his own image in them, being completely unconscious of himself. He was the least narcissistic person I have ever known. As he was indifferent to himself; he never chose friends because they were like him, or because they were the opposite of him, or because they could enrich him with thoughts and ideas he hadn't got. He simply made friends with people with whom he found it possible to establish some kind of dialogue. When he was with anyone he was never in a position of superiority or inferiority, he was always equal to the other person.

I kept the idea of the enquiry, which in any case was fairly vague in my mind for the future. What I liked about it, yet at the same time what worried me about it, was the name of Ardigò; and the memory of the very likeable man who had come to my house that day made me feel cheerful.

Time went by, and I heard no more of the job. I thought that it must have gone up in smoke like so many other plans. But the other day *Unità* published a photocopy of a typewritten sheet from the television people, giving a number of proposals, among them this enquiry on women. My name was written there, and so was Ardigò's. Beside them, in ink, was a remark expressing puzzlement. "Two Communists," it said. The whole thing made me feel profoundly amazed. I was also very pleased. Why I was so pleased, I don't know.

From *Unità* I learnt that Ardigò had an official position in the Christian Democrat Party. Actually, I didn't even know that about him, either. Then I wondered what I knew exactly about myself, as far as politics was concerned. I must admit that I know nothing very definite. The only thing I know with absolute certainty is that I know nothing about politics. In my life I have joined a political party on two occasions. Once, the Partito d'Azione. Another time, the Communist Party. Both times it was a mistake. As I understood nothing about politics, it was stupid to pretend I did and to go to meetings and carry a party card. So long as I live, I ought never to belong to any party. If I were asked how I should like a country to be governed, I wouldn't honestly know what to say. My political thinking is pretty rough and tangled, elementary and confused. This often makes me feel that the people I love despise me. They think that my poverty of thought as far as politics is concerned means that I am frivolous, unserious, obviously ignorant. They think it in silence, but I am oppressed by the weight of their scorn. If, faced with this stern silence, I were to try and justify myself, the words I would find would be grotesquely clumsy and futile. And yet I am certain that there ought to be room in the world for people who, like me, don't understand politics and who, if they did talk politics, would say only banal, stupid things, which means that the best thing they can do is hardly ever express an opinion of any kind. Sometimes, you have to say "yes" or "no." But I should like to confine myself to "yes" or "no." And as I have spoken of Felice Balbo, I will say that I am grateful to him for never having despised me, for never having been surprised at my political ignorance or scornful of it; I am immensely grateful to him for having accepted me for what I am and for having understood. First I followed him into the Communist Party, then out of it. I did everything he did, thinking that he understood politics and that I didn't. And yet with him I never had the feeling that I was beneath him, that he was superior, that I was submitting to a stronger personality. It was understood between us that he understood and knew about a great many things, and that I didn't. But this made no difference: we were equals. In my memories of the years I spent in the Communist Party, in my memories of meetings and committees, his figure is always there. Perhaps for this reason I am pleased to be called a Communist, because I remember the years when Balbo and I were there.

As far as the two parties I belonged to are concerned, one of which has long ceased to exist, I have kept some obscure, underground, visceral links with them, which I could not make clear in words but which have no basis in reason, and no relationship with the choices reason makes, but rise from the depths like affections. And I should like to add that if there was a revolution some day and I had to make a political choice, I would much rather be killed than kill someone. This is one of the few political thoughts my mind is ever able to formulate.[4]

SINIBALDI The statement "I know nothing about politics," as pronounced by Natalia Ginzburg, who is, let's remember, a member of Parliament, is a surprising admission. Vittorio Foa, a great politician, once wrote how important it is for Natalia Ginzburg to say, "I know nothing about politics"; how true and false it is, what a rich way it is of listening to politics. So I'll ask her to talk again about Felice Balbo, because she has returned often to this important philosopher.

GINZBURG Yes. I'll read a short piece I once wrote about him:

His relationships with his fellow men were never paternal and protective or consolatory or charitable, even if at times a person's unhappiness might make him feel compassion. As to the unhap-

piness of the individual he could always find an explanation in the
universal condition. If asked, he would sometimes give practical
advice, but it was always eccentric. Still, his attention to the individual was total and profound; but it was clear that he was not
there to help and administer cures or to be cured and helped. He
was there to find a way, along with the next man, through a zone
that was not commonly visited, a zone where the only important
thing was to separate what was true from what was false and to
look closely at what was true. There was no room in such a zone
for the personal and private wounds, the frustrations and depri-
vations suffered by him or by his fellow man. There was no room
for private sadnesses and their causes, stemming from some distant past and now tucked away in the most hidden wrinkles of the
spirit: they seemed totally without importance. The attention that
he gave to others was the exact same kind and quality of attention
that he gave to himself; he made no distinction between others
and himself. He would not caress or sooth either his own wounds
or those of others; he would simply go toward, and lead others
toward, a place where there was neither the time nor the space
to indulge oneself or cry over private concerns. After talking with
him you would find that although your anguish and your own personal complications were still intact, you were not being dragged
down into the confusion they created on a daily basis. The hurt
they caused did not go away, but you found yourself looking on
like someone staring at the turmoil of a restless sea from the bridge
of a ship. The nastiness, meanness of spirit, the wrongdoings and
moral laxity of his fellow men did not escape him; he saw through
the ambition and all the most spiteful, twisted and sordid tricks
of which his fellow man was capable. For although he was naive
and unprepared when it came to practical living, he was astute
and anything but naive in his knowledge of men. But if he had
the chance to talk to someone, their faults and vices were never
so off-putting as to make him refuse to engage in a discussion.
Any vileness he found he would simply clamber over, not out of
tolerance but with an astounding indifference, driven by the need
to walk with others in a zone where there was neither the time
nor the space for vileness and wretchedness. I've never met anyone
so little concerned that he might contaminate or sully himself in
the company of someone else. If this was an error on his part, I
couldn't say; but I can't ever see him behaving otherwise. If he

ever expressed hatred or contempt for someone, it was usually for people or groups of people whom he had never seen or who were outside his circle. When someone was in front of him, he was incapable of hating that person, and he was incapable of not talking to someone who clearly wanted to ask him something. His time and his health, the immense fatigue that would come over him in the evening, after he had spent the day thinking, talking, and writing, these were problems of which he was unaware, because to think in the company of others was his job.

When people have died, we suddenly understand where they fit in the landscape, as it were, of the universe. There are people who stay in our memory as rocks, others who are there as trees, others who are like gardens, or clouds or hills, or rivers. Balbo was certainly like a river. A river: he doesn't care, and it is no concern of his what kind of beasts come to drink there; he doesn't know how much they may sully his waters, whether his visitors are packs of wolves, flocks of sheep, women rinsing out their washing, children playing. A river cannot deny its waters to a living soul. It only knows that it must head toward the sea.

SINIBALDI Perhaps we can complete the picture of Balbo by saying that he was one of those figures—not so rare at the time—who was a Communist Catholic. How is it that you, neither Catholic nor Communist, came to be attracted to this double "belonging," you who came from a total "nonbelonging"?

GINZBURG I became a Communist and . . . well, now I feel Jewish and Catholic, both.

SINIBALDI You turned your childhood nonbelonging into a dual citizenship?

GINZBURG Yes, into a dual citizenship . . . yes.

SINIBALDI This is very strange, perhaps something we can come back to. And Felice Balbo, how did he respond to these religious awakenings in you? Did he direct you, help you?

GINZBURG Well, that's hard to say, because I would talk about everything, and he was someone you could really talk to about everything. He would give me practical advice. He would tell me to go to the Communist cell, and I went but got bored.

SINIBALDI To the cell: for the sake of our younger listeners, that means one of the bases of the Communist Party.

GINZBURG Yes, but I found it boring in the cell. Then, Felice moved away from the Communist Party.

SINIBALDI Why did you find it boring in the cell? To belong to a cell—wasn't this every left-wing intellectual's dream at the time?

GINZBURG Yes, but I found it extremely boring.

SINIBALDI Which cell did Felice Balbo, send you to?

GINZBURG Various ones, but there was a cell in the publishing house.

SINIBALDI Which comprised practically everyone in the publishing house.

GINZBURG Yes . . . yes, we would all go, it was inside the building. I think you went down some stairs.

SINIBALDI [He laughs] Under the stairs of the publishing house there was a Communist Party cell! We'll talk more about this with Giulio Einaudi, because this confirms all the accusations and fears of the enemies of the publishing house, doesn't it? To think there was a cell under the stairs!

GINZBURG Yes, but I think there were cells everywhere for anyone who wanted to be a Communist. It wasn't peculiar to the publishing house.

SINIBALDI [He laughs] No doubt. Let's get back to your books. In those first months following the war, you were writing a short novel, a long story, It Happened Like This, which came out in 1947. It evokes the climate of the time, not like the enthusiasts who expressed great faith in the future, but another sentiment that dates to that era: a kind of distrust that was almost materialistic, founded on an analysis that centered on the psychological makeup and sufferings of your characters. It is a story, you wrote, "submerged in smoke, rain, and mists." You also said that while you were writing The Road to the City, you had a kind of energy, that you wanted to wound with every phrase, you wanted each phrase to contain a lash of a whip or a slap.

GINZBURG Yes.

SINIBALDI Whereas when you wrote It Happened Like This, you were so unhappy that you had lost all desire or strength to render slaps or lashes or do the violent things that you associated with the idea of writing. Is it from these feelings that the bitter story of It Happened Like This was born?

GINZBURG Yes, this story starts with a shot. "I shot him in the eyes." This too, perhaps, was a chance beginning; I was starting off from a beginning that was rather dependent on chance.

SINIBALDI But which was in the air. In '46, the idea of a gun shot, of a shooting—

53

GINZBURG —was certainly in the air. I had in my mind at the time a novel that I had read without any commas. I can't remember the author, it was called *Mother's Cry*—I read it in Italian because I don't know English . . . oh no, I read it in French. I didn't like it that much, but it gave me a kind of push. I wanted to write a novel that was a bit like that one. It was the story of a woman who had a son who went to the electric chair. I don't remember the rest—I never reread it.

SINIBALDI Fortunate that you didn't write a novel without any commas!

GINZBURG No, because later, while I was writing, they came to me, the commas.

SINIBALDI Well, this rebellion is healthy. *It Happened Like This*, in spite of all the depression and the climate of despair, of prostration, is a very violent novel.

GINZBURG Violent but very sad. I thought later that, had I been happier, perhaps I would have written a better novel. It was a novel—

SINIBALDI —with unhappiness that turns in on itself too much.

GINZBURG Unhappiness too much turned in on itself, yes. And also, so it seemed, when you are happier you invent more as you write, whereas when you're unhappier you invent less. The imagination is less fervent.

SINIBALDI Because one is more oppressed by things, and it is things one writes about, rather than imagination.

GINZBURG It's things, yes.

SINIBALDI The protagonist is an unhappy woman, a wife whose husband has been unfaithful.

GINZBURG A passive woman.

SINIBALDI These are common female figures, seemingly complimentary to the inept males you describe. Was it really so bleak?

GINZBURG Yes, passive women and inept men.

SINIBALDI I know that you have already shied away from explaining why the human picture was so bleak.

GINZBURG I don't know how to explain it. I think I have a lot of passivity inside of me, and I also have the opposite, or so I think. The inept men . . . I don't know.

SINIBALDI We've already said it: a reaction to the energetic and intelligent men, a hidden wish to have less energetic, less intelligent men.

GINZBURG Yes, perhaps.

MIRELLA FULVI That's quite a far-fetched psychoanalytic reading, though . . .

SINIBALDI *It Happened Like This* is a long, largely internalized monologue by a girl, a woman.

GINZBURG Yes, it has almost no dialogue.

SINIBALDI Dialogue will be your new discovery, as we will see, in the fifties, in your books.

GINZBURG Yes. In *The Road to the City* there was dialogue. But when I wrote *It Happened Like This* I was depressed. When I'm depressed, dialogue doesn't come to me in the same way.

SINIBALDI We are discovering the characteristics of literary depression: not much invention or dialogue, then.

GINZBURG Yes, yes, at least for me.

SINIBALDI People have spoken of a passion you had for neorealism. What did you think of that poetic theory, that style?

GINZBURG Well, at the time it appealed to me. I wanted to get away from how literature had been during the Fascist years, that is, distant, removed . . .

SINIBALDI Emphatic, rhetorical.

GINZBURG Yes, and removed from real life. Neorealism seemed to be a way of getting close to life, of getting inside life, inside reality.

SINIBALDI This got a mixed reception from critics of the time. There's an old review from the journal *Rinascita* written by Laura Ingrao, which I was showing you a while ago.[5] It talks of an American-style writing technique. And someone else wrote, "You feel [Ginzburg] has read too many Americans." There were also some moralistic Catholic critiques that accused you of having inherited an amorality so often seen in the stories of the great American literary tradition of this century—perhaps Faulkner. I'm not sure whom your Catholic enemy had in mind.

GINZBURG [*She laughs*] I don't know. I don't remember this review.

SINIBALDI It's in one of the anthologies about you. The review by Laura Ingrao, on the other hand, in *Rinascita*, was interesting because at a certain point she said, "It's clear that if with so much of today's prose we are left wondering 'why?' here we feel that whoever wrote *just had to write*." She recognized that finally you had come out of the nightmare of "chance" writing. To say of a text that it clearly had to be written means that it is not a chance event. Were you aware of that?

GINZBURG Yes, yes, I was aware of it, of course. I wrote the story very quickly. Pavese was writing *The Comrade*, I think, at the same time.

But I wanted to detach myself a bit from Pavese's methods, I wanted to move away slightly from his influence.

SINIBALDI Yes, *The Comrade* came out in '47, so I imagine you both wrote together.

GINZBURG Yes, so it was . . . yes.

SINIBALDI That is, you were both writing while working at Einaudi.

GINZBURG Yes, we used to write at work. [*She laughs*] But we did work very hard. We worked extremely hard, but then sometimes we would write these novels.

SINIBALDI I ask because people have always wondered how come Pavese managed to write all those novels, working all day.

GINZBURG Pavese was such a hard worker. Such a hard worker. I wasn't as hardworking as he, but I worked a lot, too. He would come into the office on Sundays, too, if he wanted to do his own writing or just work. You see, there wasn't a strict pattern.

SINIBALDI To the working day?

GINZBURG No, no.

SINIBALDI Now let's look at the epic model that fascinated you as a child, the great literature of the nineteenth century. This left its mark on your liveliest novel, the one that offers the richest range of characters and plot, *All Our Yesterdays*, published in 1952. The novel in which, on the one hand, memory has the lead role—or rather, there's a gradual discovery of memory in your narrative. This represents a fundamental stage, because it is the memory of the Resistance, of events, of the maturing, politically speaking, of a generation.

GINZBURG Yes, everything . . . it's all made up, but with autobiography going out one door then coming back in through the window, yes.

SINIBALDI All made up, but every now and then there enters a rather brusque reality.

GINZBURG Yes, there's no doubt about that. Besides, the village in the second half is totally Pizzoli.

SINIBALDI A kind of self-internment, then? The characters—the couple, the young wife and the older, more educated husband—go there without anyone obliging them to.

GINZBURG There you have a positive man, there's a man . . .

SINIBALDI The first positive hero, at last, of your books.

GINZBURG This man called Cenzo Rena is definitely a positive hero.

SINIBALDI How come a positive hero finally appears?

GINZBURG Who knows? I don't know.

SINIBALDI This is the extract we've chosen from *All Our Yesterdays:*

One evening as they were just finishing supper Emanuele arrived with Danilo. It was the first time Danilo had set foot in the house, and Concettina went very red, with red patches even on her neck. Concettina was peeling an orange and pretended to be deeply absorbed in peeling it, and she did not look at Danilo, and Danilo threw her one quick, knowing glance and went on talking to Ippolito who was saying that he had been expecting him for some time. Signora Maria was very frightened, because Danilo had always frightened her, with his mania for standing quite still in front of their gate. Danilo and Concettina had met at a dance, and after that they had sometimes gone for a walk together, but Concettina said he had made a vulgar remark to her, a very vulgar remark; Signora Maria asked what it was but Concettina would not repeat it. He came from quite a high-class family, but they had become impoverished and his mother was reduced to working as a cashier in a bakery. And there was a sister who was by no means a steady character. Concettina had given him to understand that she did not wish to see him anymore. But he remained unconvinced and was always standing in front of the gate, and when Concettina went out he always walked behind her, without speaking but with a threatening look on his face, Concettina said. And now Emanuele had brought him into the house and Ippolito had said that he had been expecting him for quite a long time, and there he was, sitting quietly at the table, peeling an orange that Ippolito had given him. But when he had eaten the orange Ippolito told him to go up with him into the sitting room; Emanuele, on the other hand, stayed to try and convince Signora Maria that Danilo was a charming young man, the best in the world, and that it was quite impossible that he should have made a vulgar remark to Concettina, that probably there had been a misunderstanding. And it was not true that his sister was not a steady character; he, Emanuele, had seen the sister and she had seemed to him a very steady character indeed; in any case he had a whole pack of sisters, from sixteen years old to three months. But Concettina said there had been no misunderstanding at all, it had really been a very vulgar remark. She did not want Danilo in the house, and she was very angry; she rushed out of the room, banging the door. Emanuele and Ippolito stayed talking to Danilo in the sitting room until late, and Signora Maria had left her work there and wanted to go and fetch it, but Giustino told her she must leave it and that it was impossible to disturb them. And after that evening Danilo took to arriving at any moment with Emanuele, and Ippolito would shut himself up with them in the sitting room. And Ippolito told Concettina that he would receive anyone in the house that he wanted to, and Concettina started sobbing loudly, and then Emanuele in order to comfort her took her to the cinema to see *Anna Karenina* with Greta Garbo, and when they came back Concettina was comforted; she always liked so much to see Greta Garbo and imagined that she was just a little like her, because Greta Garbo, too, had no bosom. "This Danilo has got a real crush on Concettina," said Anna to Giustino. She had learned from her school friends to say "a crush," and now she was pleased when she had an opportunity to use the word. But then Giustino said that Danilo didn't care two pence about Concettina and that when he stood in front of the gate he did it to annoy her. Danilo had quite other ideas in his head. Anna asked what ideas Danilo had. Giustino wrinkled up his nose and his lips and brought his face close to hers with a more and more ugly grimace upon it. "Politics," he whispered into her ear, and ran away.

"Politics," thought Anna. She walked about the garden, amongst Signora Maria's rose trees and repeated the word to herself. She was a plump girl, pale and indolent, dressed in a pleated skirt and faded blue pullover, and not very tall for her fourteen years. "Politics," she repeated slowly, and now all at once she seemed to understand: this was why Danilo had taken to coming so often to the house—because he was talking politics with Ippolito and Emanuele. She seemed to understand about the sitting room, and the sentences in German, and Ippolito stroking his face, and his restless eyes that were always looking for something. They were talking politics in the sitting room, they were once again doing a dangerous, secret thing, as the book of memoirs had been. They wanted to overthrow the Fascists, to begin a revolution. Her father had always said that the Fascists must be overthrown, that he himself would be the first to mount the barricades, on the day of the revolution. He used to say that it would be the finest day of his life. And then his whole life had gone past without that day happening. Anna now pictured herself upon the barricades, with Ippolito and Danilo, firing off a rifle and singing. She went very quietly up to the sitting room and slowly pushed the door open. They were all three sitting on the carpet, with a big bundle of newspapers in front of them, and they got a great fright when they saw her coming in. Emanuele threw Danilo's coat over the newspapers and shouted at her to go away and as she was going she heard Danilo say to Ippolito that he was a fool not to have locked the door.[6]

SINIBALDI We chose this extract for a reason. It's about a group of friends, young people tied by the normal, chance bonds of friendship who then consolidate these bonds first in a kind of political solidarity, then in a political conspiracy.

GINZBURG Clandestine activity, yes.

SINIBALDI It is a novel about the Resistance. So, how come you decided to talk about this? Were you influenced by the fact that, at the time, people were writing that kind of novel? Some great novels were written . . .

GINZBURG I really wanted to write a novel about the war as I remembered it. It felt like I was writing in octaves, because there were these long phrases, there were no dialogues, few commas.

SINIBALDI Ah, right: you were getting closer perhaps to the ideal of that terrifying narrator with no commas.

GINZBURG I had no particular models in my mind. It was just something that from the first word to the last I wanted to do.

SINIBALDI Once again . . . the end of "chance" writing.

GINZBURG Not by chance. Yes, it really was the end of writing by chance. And the novel turned out to be very long. I had always written short novels; this one was quite long.

SINIBALDI You once said that the impulse to write short novels had something of an autobiographical source: your mother, when she read long novels, would complain, "What a lot of hot air." And you've said more than once that it was your mother's influence that made you cut novels down. What was going on here, then: a need to pull away from the maternal influence?

GINZBURG From my mother's influence and from my brothers' who would tell me to be quiet when I talked. So I thought I had to say things quickly, with few words, in order to be heard.

SINIBALDI I want to believe these explanations; but they don't seem enough to me. Was there not, when you wrote this long, vast, epic novel, was there not also a kind of new faith in yourself?

GINZBURG Well, maybe so.

SINIBALDI More important than the need to pull away from brothers who would shout you down.

GINZBURG Yes; and it seems a different novel from It Happened Like This, because there's a brighter light inside it, even if dramas, tragedies occur. But I had come out of my depression.

SINIBALDI A review of it came out in Belfagor, Luigi Russo's journal, which was blatantly left-wing. The signature at the end will be a surprise because it is Pietro Citati.[7]

Having started off with the "short novel," thin on characters and closed in its own absorbed rhythm, Natalia Ginzburg has suddenly arrived, with great poise and a steady breath, at the novel that is teeming with characters and goings-on. All Our Yesterdays: a period, no less, in recent Italian history, from the prewar period to 1945, intertwined with the events in the lives of two bourgeois families. But the protagonist is still the one of It Happened Like This; and the lyrical core of the novel is still entrusted to a continuous thread of psychological absence and a prolonged, youthful awe, a clear sign of a fundamental inability to live. A figure that we have met and come to know so many times before: closed in her emptiness, her silence, in her escapist dreams, and not even capable of expressing precise feelings, but passively yielding to the will and force of events. Where [Ginzburg's] writing has become more colorful, has extended, is above all in a lively and colorful "minor" world of fools, little men and old ladies: the Turkish carpet seller who feels the cold, the mushroom picker, the marchioness with her boa, the piano teacher with his Latin grammar . . . But not even here are we anchored to reality, and that psychology and these little figures combine in an atmosphere that is part fairy tale, part grotesque, part funny, part dreamlike, with just the slightest hint of a gentle, crepuscular decline. An unreal fantasy world where the problematic and idealistic Cenzo Rena may also seem like a strange scarecrow, and facts unfold like a nursery rhyme, with no signs of "structure," everything depending on powerful triggers of the memory running through a kind of "continuous song." It was no doubt the American models that inspired the author to abandon a traditional syntax in favor of the purely coordinating link (the "and . . . and . . . and"); but it seems clear to me that, as for tone and taste, the effective ties are more figurative than literary, and we are reminded of that good-natured painting style that we associate with the great Henri Rousseau and that can sometimes be found even in those collections of children's drawings, which everybody knows . . .

SINIBALDI That was Citati. Astute. We happened to choose the first part of the review; later, in the second part, he had some rather harsh criticism.

GINZBURG Harsh; I don't remember them.

SINIBALDI He said that the truth was—

GINZBURG The truth was, I wrote about nothing.

SINIBALDI [He laughs] No, but that to attempt to tell the story of those years is a hopeless ambition.

GINZBURG That was probably true.

SINIBALDI No, he said that the "continuous song" was impossible, the way you adopted a low note in your tone and your rigorous style. Did All Our Yesterdays give rise to a lot of debate?

GINZBURG Um . . . I don't think so . . . it wasn't a great success. It received a good review by De Feo, I remember. And Elsa Morante liked the novel. She called and told me she liked it.

SINIBALDI And Niccolò Gallo liked it. Niccolò Gallo is another of the figures relegated to the second tier when we reconstruct those years. And yet, like Felice Balbo, he is an important figure.

GINZBURG Very important.

SINIBALDI Perhaps because they are figures of great listeners rather than great creators.

GINZBURG Yes; but Felice Balbo has perhaps left more behind, he left a fat book.[8] But Niccolò Gallo was also very important.

SINIBALDI As a reader, as an advisor?

GINZBURG As a reader, as a listener, as a moral figure, he was extremely important.

SINIBALDI Let's listen to what Niccolò Gallo wrote, as he reviewed the literature of '53.[9] He said it had been a year in a minor tone. But then, considering the titles he mentions, we see that it is the year in which Primo Levi's *If This Is a Man* came out. As did the *Memorie di prigionia* (Memories of imprisonment) by Giampiero Carocci, and Cassola's *I vecchi compagni* (Old friends). It's the year in which *The Bay Is Not Naples* by Anna Maria Ortese came out, *The Sergeant in the Snow* by Rigoni

61

Stern, *The Mad Women of Magliano* by Tobino, Gadda's *Novelle dal ducato in fiamme* (Stories from the dukedom in flames), Alba de Céspedes; and an extraordinary story, a posthumous one, Silvio D'Arzo's *Casa d'altri* (Other peoples' home).

GINZBURG All in the same year? It wasn't bad, then!

SINIBALDI If we took another year we would probably have a similar impression. This is the short extract that Niccolò Gallo devotes to you in his review:

> Keeping the gray and unadorned tone with which we have come to recognize her storytelling, Natalia Ginzburg has arrived with *All Our Yesterdays* (Einaudi, 1952) on the threshold of a huge novel. We watch the events in the lives of the young people who make up a family unfold from the prewar years until the German occupation, with the thoughtful detachment of a chronicle enlivened and colored by continuous excitement. If Ginzburg seems to have lost some of the tension of It *Happened Like This* and some of the incisive firmness of Valentino, in return she has managed to compose a unified sequence of events in which characters, situations, and towns are placed along a harmonious distribution of levels.

An opinion that must have pleased you. At that time Gallo was a very influential critic.

GINZBURG I didn't know him then. I got to know him much later.

SINIBALDI What importance does a reader have? Let's take Niccolò Gallo as an example of a reader and adviser. What does it mean to have a critic nearby, who will read your manuscript and be always available as a yardstick? Is it important for you? I mean, do you take a lot of notice of a first reading, of first reactions?

GINZBURG Ah, it's so important! So was Niccolò Gallo. I've also written about him.

SINIBALDI Yes, you wrote a tribute called "Niccolò" in your essays.

GINZBURG And Garboli wrote something very lovely about him in this latest book called *Falbalas*.

SINIBALDI As we're talking about the 1950s, we can move on to a central theme in your life, your work at Einaudi.

GINZBURG And how I got in? Muscetta gave me a job. He wasn't there.

SINIBALDI "He" is Giulio Einaudi, who in the meantime has come into the studio and whom Natalia Ginzburg has introduced in this way [*he laughs*] and whom we thank, of course. But your friendship dated from way before then: Natalia Ginzburg pretends she was taken on by Muscetta like some kind of unknown, but naturally Muscetta knew who she was.

GINZBURG Muscetta was great friends with Leone.

SINIBALDI Exactly. He was with Leone when he was arrested, for example.

GINZBURG Yes, yes, they were arrested together, and he took me on, gave me a job.

GIULIO EINAUDI Were you a full-time employee? Did you have an employment card, the whole package?

GINZBURG Not an employment card, no. Well, he gave me a salary. He paid me a lot, in fact, for those days it was a lot: seven thousand lire a month.

EINAUDI Yes, you came into the office all the time; but at that time I don't think offices were yet using—

GINZBURG No, there was no such thing as employment cards; only after the war.

SINIBALDI [*He laughs*] Perhaps, considering recent events, Giulio Einaudi wants to be very precise about administrative issues. [10]

GINZBURG No employment cards, no contracts, they weren't even discussed.

EINAUDI Nothing.

GINZBURG But . . .

EINAUDI You had a good salary.

GINZBURG The salary was good.

SINIBALDI Salary is everything, my dear Giulio. She knows that she was able to marry Leone Ginzburg because Leone Ginzburg finally got the guarantee of a salary. Her attention to this economic issue is totally understandable.

EINAUDI In which year did you get to know Muscetta and he took you on?

GINZBURG No, Muscetta I knew already. He took me on in the autumn of '44, it must have been.

EINAUDI I wasn't there.

GINZBURG No, in the autumn of '45; no, you weren't there.

EINAUDI But in the autumn of '45 weren't you in Turin?

GINZBURG No, no, that was the autumn of '44.

SINIBALDI Now let's patiently reconstruct the editorial career of Natalia Ginzburg.

GINZBURG It was the autumn of '44. He wasn't there. Then you arrived, we were still in via Monteverde. You arrived, and you phoned Muscetta.

SINIBALDI Perhaps we need to clarify why he wasn't there; it isn't that he had abandoned—

GINZBURG —No, he was a long way away.

SINIBALDI He was in the Resistance, first in Switzerland. Meanwhile the publishing house carried on, especially in Rome.

GINZBURG And when Giulio arrived, he called. Muscetta said, "But who is it?" and he said, "Don't you recognize your boss's voice?" And Muscetta said, "What boss?! I have no boss!" And Giulio said, "But it's me!"

[*Laughter*]

SINIBALDI One of your first jobs—and this would terrify anyone just starting out in editorial work—was the translation of Proust.

GINZBURG Yes, which I was already working on during internment.

SINIBALDI Yes, but all the same, to start one's working life by translating Proust . . .

GINZBURG Well, I've said it was a mad idea to give me this translation. I was young, and I had never read Proust when I started translating it.

SINIBALDI But he was a constant presence in your family. Debenedetti, one of the first Italian readers of Proust, was courting your sister.

GINZBURG He, Einaudi, and Leone had given me this translation to do, which I did . . . just the first two volumes.

SINIBALDI There's a page from this translation that we would like to hear.[11] It was broadcast by Rai for the program *Pages*. Until a few years ago, Ginzburg's was the only translation, I think, but once the rights became free . . .

GINZBURG Now there's Raboni.

SINIBALDI There are other editions now in addition to Natalia Ginzburg's translation.

EINAUDI You've compared them. What's Raboni's version like?

GINZBURG I prefer mine.

SINIBALDI Recently a rather heated cultural debate has reignited accusations (which are not by any means new) against the cultural policies of Einaudi. One of the accusations was that the publishing house functioned like a Communist dictatorship in the fifties . . . it would be the only case of cultural dictatorship in a country where there was no political dictatorship and where the government was in the hands of another party, which would make it a unique "historical monster." But I would like to start off with when you met early on: the meetings that coincide with the founding of the publishing house. Even if there is a slight difference of opinion as to its founding—Natalia Ginzburg, in a review of *Frammenti di memoria* (Fragments of memory) by Giulio Einaudi, reproached him, accused him of remembering incorrectly.[12]

GINZBURG Yes, he didn't say correctly that it had been Leone who started the publishing house and I thought he needed to make that clear.

SINIBALDI Be open, clear. That was the only disagreement.

GINZBURG Just that. And then he called Pavese in straightaway; I was there at the birth of this publishing house, which seemed to me to begin when the first volumes in the Essays series came out. Giudio told me his father [Luigi Einaudi] had advised him to take on Huizinga. To me it seems that Leone founded the publishing house; but Giulio says otherwise. But it isn't important.

SINIBALDI And for you, Giulio Einaudi, what was your first meeting with Natalia Ginzburg, do you remember?

EINAUDI Well, really, the important one is the meeting with Leone.

GINZBURG Of course.

EINAUDI . . . which she is now trying to pass off as something I am trying to make light of. I have always recognized the importance of this meeting with Leone. Five years ago, when I was in Moscow, I remember saying that Einaudi has published all the nineteenth-century Russian classics—Tolstoy, Dostoevsky—thanks to the man with whom—of course I said "with whom" . . . You said, "he founded the publishing house." No, he founded the publishing house with me. If you change it to this, I agree.

GINZBURG Yes, OK, OK.

EINAUDI The man who cofounded it with me and who was concerned with the editorial side of things—that was Leone. Then all his troubles took him far away, but even from Pizzoli he kept on sending postcards and letters, always censored, full of advice and criticism, mostly criticism, and some expressing surprise at certain books he didn't like or praising others. "Lovely, this book that's just come out: I'm really pleased, well done." He did all this to show the censors that his relationship with the publishing house was extraneous, so as not to compromise it. Lovely letters, some of them really lovely—[to *Natalia*] I can let you have copies if you like. There are lots of them, all very detailed, philological. For each book he would point out any mistakes: "Please note that here you've made a mistake." Very interesting letters.

SINIBALDI I'd like to point out that when we talk about the founding of the Einaudi publishing house, we are talking about events in the first half of the 1930s, so the occasional memory lapse . . .

EINAUDI The first half of the 1930s. Well, the second half of the thirties, too.

GINZBURG '37.

EINAUDI In Pizzoli . . .

GINZBURG '40.

EINAUDI '40. But first Leone was in prison.

GINZBURG No. He was in prison from '34 to '36. Then he came back. And you met. He told me that you met.

SINIBALDI He started working. So, Giulio Einaudi, you remember Natalia Ginzburg as a reflection of the meeting with Leone Ginzburg.

GINZBURG Yes, because—

SINIBALDI No—how does Giulio Einaudi remember it? Giulio Einaudi has to answer.

EINAUDI I don't know, I know Leone talked about Natalia, saying, "She's written some good stories; I married her, she writes good stories."

SINIBALDI These two things, "I married her" and "She's written some good stories"?

EINAUDI Yes. And then Natalia and I met later.

GINZBURG Yes, we met later. Well, no, actually I was there when you used to come over. I was present. I'd sit there quietly and listen. There was Pavese, him, Leone.

SINIBALDI So when was it that Natalia Ginzburg's importance in the publishing house became obvious?

EINAUDI Well, when you came later on . . . after Muscetta took you on.

GINZBURG But they'd given me this job, to do *À la recherche du temps perdu*, he and Leone, this . . .

EINAUDI Yes, we gave you that.

GINZBURG I had to do the whole of *Recherche du temps perdu*, which was a huge undertaking, crazy, because I didn't know . . .

EINAUDI And you translated part of it while you were interned.

GINZBURG Then I brought it to Rome and finished it there.

EINAUDI And now it's being reprinted in a famous series of writers who translate writers.

SINIBALDI Of which it was an early example.

EINAUDI Natalia is a forerunner of the idea for this series, I have to say. But now she's added a postscript to her translation, which has thrown the publishing house into confusion. They say, "What? The postscript should consist of the translator declaring that he has completed the work!" Instead, she says, "They have now published my translation in another series, the paperback series, claiming that it is to revive the text but in fact they have also made corrections to my version." And she demonstrates how hers was better, showing up these proofreaders who haven't a clue. She's right; [to Natalia] I quoted this piece of yours at the Trieste conference on translating.

GINZBURG Did you? In fact they did also correct some mistakes, and for that I'm grateful.

SINIBALDI This . . . who? Einaudi's proofreaders?

GINZBURG Yes, these proofreaders whose identity I don't know, I don't know them. They corrected some mistakes I'd made, and I'm grateful. But there were some things that—for instance, where I wrote "giovane," they wrote "giovine."[13] I mean "giovane"! I defend the right to say "giovane"!

EINAUDI And then, above all, she was offended because they didn't show her the proposed corrections; they just published them without saying a word. The fact is, this was a black period at the publishing house. There was a lot of confusion; new editorial directors kept coming and going at a crazy rate.

SINIBALDI Giulio Einaudi, if we were to sum up the importance of Natalia Ginzburg's work in the publishing house, it would be—

GINZBURG Very little.

EINAUDI Well, if you want to focus on the early 1930s, I'm rather stuck for a reply. But, for example, her role was a pivotal one in the years following the Liberation [to Natalia] when you were working in Turin with Mila and Pavese.

GINZBURG And Balbo.

EINAUDI You were defending the publishing house from these Lombard invasions, weren't you? There was no Lombard league at the time, but nevertheless Pavese defended the "Piedmonticity" of the publishing house against Elio Vittorini [from Milan]. He was fiercely opposed to Vittorini.

GINZBURG I wasn't opposed to Vittorini. Pavese was at odds with him; he would grumble because they were producing this review, Politecnico, and he said it cost too much.

SINIBALDI But it did cost too much, didn't it? Giulio Einaudi here can confirm.

EINAUDI Then over time, Natalia became part of the critical conscience of the publishing house, as "Il manifesto" was for some years for the Communist Party.

GINZBURG Ah! Maybe . . .

SINIBALDI It's a comparison you like.

EINAUDI Do you like it as a comparison?

GINZBURG Yes . . . yes.

SINIBALDI And what does it mean, "critical conscience"? I mean, how did she criticize you?

EINAUDI If there's something she doesn't like, she says so straight-away. She isn't one of those people who pretends nothing's wrong. She says it, she shouts it out, kicks up a fuss, says it on TV if she can, on the radio.

SINIBALDI And what was it that she didn't like about Einaudi?

GINZBURG For example, at a certain point they made a series for young people—

EINAUDI Ooh, ooh, ooh . . .

GINZBURG —and I wrote an article saying that it was a series of Piedmont male authors.

EINAUDI You were wrong, though, you were wrong.

GINZBURG Made up by Piedmont male authors. And Giulio Bollati[14] got very angry and wrote a retaliatory article.

EINAUDI And it was a good reply, too.

GINZBURG It was a good reply. But this series for the young . . . there wasn't even a single book by a woman, not half a woman, can you imagine? How many volumes were there, forty?

EINAUDI Fifty.

SINIBALDI And how come there were no women?

GINZBURG Because they were Piedmont males!

EINAUDI Bollati created it, he was very precise.

GINZBURG . . . Not even Virginia Woolf! Then once I criticized them for a series titled Without Fairies or Magicians, a series for children. Again I wrote an article.

EINAUDI The Munari one? Didn't you like it?

GINZBURG No. I wrote an article, because it was publicized as "a series for children without fairies or magicians." I said, "What do you mean, without fairies or magicians?!" and then I said, "But we've had Calvino's *Italian Folktales*, which are wonderful, with fairies and magicians." It's like saying, "We'll make a cake without milk, without eggs, and without butter."

EINAUDI Did you say that about the milk and butter then or is that now?

GINZBURG No, no, I said it then.

EINAUDI Are you sure?

GINZBURG Yes, yes, I remember: because I've since republished it—I think this one I've republished, but the one about the series for young people I haven't.

SINIBALDI But it's not as if your dissent got you very far.

GINZBURG No, it got me nowhere.

SINIBALDI [*He laughs*] Just like a critical conscience.

GINZBURG It got me nowhere, absolutely nowhere.

EINAUDI No, it made people think. In fact, it turned out that Bollati's series was not a great success. The first edition sold very slowly, then we dropped it.

GINZBURG Well, that wasn't my fault.

EINAUDI The truth is you were right. I was saying you were right.

FULVI Finally you've said it.

EINAUDI In particular, when we published that whole body of folktales from around the world, starting with Calvino then going on to Chinese folktales, Andersen, Grimm.

GINZBURG Once you told me off because I fought for Emma Parodi's *Grandma's Folktales*, a book that you later said did really badly.

EINAUDI We published it, but it didn't do well.

GINZBURG You said to me: "You! It did really badly!" But they were lovely, Emma Parodi's *Folktales* . . . though not as good as Calvino's *Italian Folktales*, which is a wonderful book. I find it a wonderful book.

SINIBALDI We've overlooked something important in talking about Einaudi: the vital role Cesare Pavese played in founding it as well as the role he played in Natalia Ginzburg's life. This is how she remembers him in one of the portraits of *The Little Virtues*, entitled "Portrait of a Friend":

The city that our friend loved is always the same; there have been changes, but very few—they have introduced trolley buses and made one or two subways. There are no new cinemas. The ancient monuments are always there with their familiar names, which when we repeat them awaken in us our youth and childhood. Now, we live elsewhere in a completely different, much bigger

69

city, and if we meet and talk about our own city we do so with no sense of regret that we have left it, and say that we could not live there any longer. But when we go back, simply passing through the station and walking in the misty avenues is enough to make us feel we have come home; and the sadness with which the city fills us every time we return lies in this feeling that we are at home and, at the same time, that we have no reason to stay here; because here, in our own home, our own city, the city in which we spent our youth, so few things remain alive for us, and we are oppressed by a throng of memories and shadows.

Besides, our city is by its nature a melancholy place. On winter mornings it has its own smell of the station and soot, diffused through all its streets and avenues; if we arrive in the morning we find it gray with fog, pervaded by that distinctive smell. Sometimes a pale sun filters through the fog and dyes the heaps of snow and bare tree branches rose and lilac; in the streets and avenues the snow is shoveled into little heaps, but the parks are still buried beneath their thick, undisturbed blanket, which lies, a finger thick, on the deserted benches and round the fountain rims: the clock by the horse track is stopped at a quarter to eleven, as it has been since time immemorial. There is a hill on the other side of the river and that, too, is white with snow, but marked here and there with reddish bushes; on the top of the hill a circular, orange-colored building that used to be the Balilla National Opera stands like a tower. If there is a little sun to catch the glass dome of the Automobile Showrooms and make the river flow with a green glitter beneath its stone bridges, the city can seem, for a moment, pleasant and friendly; but that is a fleeting impression. The city's essential nature is melancholy; the river loses itself in the distance and disappears in a horizon of violet mists, which make you think of sunsets at midday, and at any moment you can breathe in that same dark, industrial smell of soot and hear the whistle of the trains.

And now it occurs to us that our city resembles the friend whom we have lost and who loved it; it is, as he was, industrious, stamped with a frown of stubborn, feverish activity; and it is simultaneously listless and inclined to spend its time idly dreaming. Wherever we go in the city that resembles him we feel that our friend lives again; on every corner and at every turning it seems that we could suddenly see his tall figure in its dark half-belted coat, his face hidden by the collar, his hat pulled down over his eyes. Stubborn and solitary our friend walked with his long tread throughout the city; he hid himself away in remote, smoky cafés where he would immediately slip off his coat and hat but keep on the pale, ugly scarf that was carelessly flung about his neck; he twisted strands of his long brown hair around his fingers and then, quick as lightning, pushed the strands back. He filled page after page with his quick, broad handwriting, crossing out furiously as he went; and in his poetry he celebrated the city:

> Questo è il giorno che salgono le nebbie dal fiume
> Nella bella città, in mezzo a prati e colline,
> E la sfumano come un ricordo . . .
> [This is the day when mists rise from the river
> In the beautiful city set among meadows and hills,
> And they make it shadowy as a memory . . .]

When we return to the city or when we think of it his poems echo in our ears; and we no longer know whether they are good poems or not, because they have become so much a part of us, and so strongly reflect for us the image of our youth, of those far-off days when we heard them for the first time recited by the living voice of our friend, and we discovered with astonishment that it is possible to make poetry even out of our gray, heavy, unpoetic city.

Our friend lived in the city as an adolescent, and he lived in the same way until the end. His days were extremely long and full of time, like an adolescent's; he knew how to find time to study and to write, to earn his living and to wander idly through the streets he loved; whereas we, who staggered from laziness to frantic activity and back again, wasted our time trying to decide whether we were lazy or industrious. For many years he did not want to submit to office hours or accept a definite job; but when he did agree to sit behind a desk in an office he became a meticulous employee and a tireless worker: even so, he set aside an ample margin of free time for himself—his meals were quickly over, he ate very little and never slept.

At times he was very unhappy, but for a long time we thought that he would be cured of this unhappiness when he decided to become an adult; his unhappiness seemed like that of a boy—the absent-minded, voluptuous melancholy of a boy who has not yet got his feet on the ground and who lives in a sterile, solitary world of his dreams.

Sometimes, during the evening, he would come in search of us; then he just sat, pale, with his scarf about his neck, twisting strands of hair around his fingers or crumpling a piece of paper; throughout the whole evening he would not say a single word or answer any of our questions. Suddenly, at last, he would snatch up his overcoat and leave. Then we were ashamed and asked ourselves if our company had disappointed him, if he had hoped to cheer himself up by being with us and had been unsuccessful; or perhaps he had simply wanted to spend an evening in silence beneath a lamp that was not his own.

However, conversation with him was never easy, even when he seemed happy; but a meeting with him in which just a few words were exchanged could be far more stimulating than with anyone else. In his company we became more intelligent; we felt compelled to articulate whatever was best and most serious in us, and we got rid of commonplace notions, imprecise thoughts, incoherent ideas.

We often felt ashamed when we were with him, because we did not know how to be serious like him, or modest like him, or generous and unselfish like him. He treated us, his friends, in a brusque way, and he did not overlook any of our faults; but if we were upset or ill he immediately became as solicitous as a mother. On principle he refused to get to know new people; but sometimes he would be expansive and affectionate, full of appointments and plans, with someone completely unexpected—someone who was even rather contemptible—and whom he had never seen before. If we happened to remark that this person was in many ways unpleasant or despicable he used to say he was well aware of that, because he always liked to know everything and never allowed us the satisfaction of telling him something new: but he never explained why he acted in such a welcoming, intimate way with this person and, on the other hand, refused his friendship to others who deserved it much more, and we never discovered the reason. From time to time he became curious about someone who, he thought, was very elegant, and he would see a great deal of this person; perhaps he thought he could use these people in his novels; but he was mistaken in his judgments of social refinement and he often mistook bottle glass for crystal; in this, but only in this, he was very naïve. But though he made mistakes about social refinement no one could deceive him when it came to spiritual or cultural refinement.

He had a cautious, reserved way of shaking hands—a few fingers were extended and withdrawn; a secretive, parsimonious way of taking his tobacco from its pouch and filling his pipe; and if he knew that we needed money he had a sudden, brusque way of giving it to us—so brusque and sudden that we were left rather bewildered. He used to say that he felt he should be careful with the money he had and that it hurt him to part with it, but once it was gone he didn't give a damn about it. If we were separated from him he neither wrote to us nor answered our letters, or he answered with a few, flat, defensive phrases; he said the reason was that he did not know how to feel affection for friends when they were a long way off; he did not want to suffer because of their absence and he quickly buried the thought of them.

He never had a wife or children or a house of his own. He lived with a married sister who loved him and whom he loved, but when he was with his family he behaved in his usual uncouth way and his manners were those of a boy or a stranger. Sometimes he came to our houses and then he would scrutinize the children we were bringing up, the families we had made for ourselves, with a puzzled, good-natured frown: he too thought of having a family but he thought of it in a way that with the passing of the years became more and more complicated and tortuous—so tortuous that it was impossible for him to bring the idea to a simple conclusion. Over the years he had built up such a tangled and inexorable system of ideas and principles that he was unable to carry through the simplest project, and the more forbidden and impossible he made the attainment of some simple reality the deeper his desire to master it became, twining itself in ever more complicated tangles like some suffocating species of vegetation. For this reason he was often unhappy and we would have liked to help him, but he never allowed us to utter a word of pity or make any gesture of sympathy; we even imitated his behavior and refused his sympathy when we were depressed. Although he taught us many things he was not a mentor for us because we saw all too clearly the absurd convolutions of the thoughts in which he imprisoned his simple nature; we wanted to teach him something, too—how to live in a more elementary, less suffocating way. But we were never able to teach him anything, because as soon as we tried to set out our arguments he would lift his hand and say that he was already well aware of all that.

In his last years his face was lined and furrowed, laid waste by mental torment; but his build and figure retained their adolescent gracefulness to the end. In his last years he became a famous writer, but this had no effect at all on his secretive habits, nor on the modesty of his behavior, nor on the scrupulous humility with which he carried out his everyday work. When we asked him if he enjoyed being famous he gave a proud smirk and said that he had always expected to be; sometimes a shrewd, proud smirk—childish and spiteful—used to flash across his face and disappear. But because he had always expected it, it gave him no pleasure when it came, since as soon as he had something he was incapable of loving or enjoying it.

He used to say that he knew his art so thoroughly that it was impossible he should discover any further secret in it, and because it could not promise him any more secrets it no longer interested him. He told us, his friends, that we had no more secrets for him and that we bored him profoundly; we felt humiliated by the fact that we bored him, but we were unable to tell him that we saw only too clearly where his mistake lay—in his refusal to love the daily current of existence, which flows on evenly and apparently without secrets. He had not yet mastered day-to-day reality, but this—for which he felt a simultaneous desire and disgust—was impregnable and forbidden to him: and so he could only look at it as if from an infinite distance.

He died in the summer. In summer our city is deserted and seems very large, clear, and echoing, like an empty city square; the sky has a milky pallor, limpid but not luminous; the river flows as level as a street and gives off neither humidity nor freshness. Sudden clouds of dust rise from the streets; huge carts loaded with sand pass by on their way from the river; the asphalt of the main avenue is littered with pebbles that bake in the tar. Outside the cafés, beneath their fringed umbrellas, the little tables are deserted and red-hot.

None of us were there. He chose to die on an ordinary, stiflingly hot day in August, and he chose a room in a hotel near the station;

he wanted to die like a stranger in the city to which he belonged. He had imagined his death in a poem written many, many years before:

> Non sarà necessario lasciare il letto.
> Solo l'alba entrerà nella stanza vuota.
> Basterà la finestra a vestire ogni cosa
> D'un chiarore tranquillo, quasi una luce.
> Poserà un'ombra scarna sul volto supino.
> I ricordi saranno dei grumi d'ombra
> Appiattati cosí come vecchia brace
> Nel camino. Il ricordo sarà la vampa
> Che ancor ieri mordeva negli occhi spenti.
> [It will not be necessary to get up from the bed.
> Only the morning will enter the empty room.
> The window will be sufficient to clothe everything
> With a quiet clarity, like light.
> It will cast a thin shadow on his face where it lies.
> What will be remembered are clots of shadow
> Flattened like old ashes
> In the fireplace. Memory will be the flame
> That yesterday flared in his dead eyes.]

A short time after his death we went on a trip into the hills. There were inns by the roadside with pergolas covered in ripening grapes, games of bocce, heaps of bicycles; there were farms growing corn, and cut grass spread out on sacks to dry; it was the landscape just beyond the city, at the end of autumn, which he loved. We watched the September night come up over the low hills and ploughed fields. We were all close friends and had known each other for many years, we were people who had always worked and thought together. As happens among those who have suffered a misfortune together, we tried to love each other all the more, to look after each other, because we felt that he, in some mysterious way of his own, had always looked after us and protected us. On that hillside he was more present than ever.

> Ogni occhiata che torna, conserva un gusto
> Di erba e cose impregnate di sole a sera
> Sulla spiaggia. Conserva un fiato di mare.
> Come un mare notturno è quest'ombra vaga

Di ansie e brividi antichi, che il cielo sfiora
E ogni sera ritorna. Le voci morte
Assomigliano al frangersi di quel mare.
[As it comes back, every glance keeps some quality
Of the grass and of the things on the beach
Suffused by the evening sun. It keeps a breath of the sea.
This indistinct shadow compounded of anxieties
And ancient shudderings is like a nocturnal sea
On which the sky rests lightly, and which
Returns each evening. The voices of the dead
Are like the breaking of that sea.][15]

SINIBALDI A portrait without a name, but in it we recognize Cesare Pavese. His death in 1950 is a dividing line in the history of Einaudi, not only because of the sense of loss, which, I think, everyone in the publishing house felt. Perhaps it marked the end of the heroic era of the publishing house and the beginning of the political adventure that nowadays is the cause of so much debate. Let's start with this date, 1950; Cesare Pavese, his death, which is also the end, symbolically, of so many hopes, illusions, bringing you up against the true reality of the 1950s, a difficult cultural reality. What changed for you?

GINZBURG Well, after Pavese's suicide we were completely lost, I think, because he did everything in the publishing house. He had an extraordinary capacity for hard work; I've never seen a person work so hard, do so many things. In my opinion he was the guiding force behind the publishing house, and apart from the great pain of having lost him, there was this sense of How would we carry on? What should we do? And I sensed this in Calvino, in Balbo, in everyone. And then soon after, Balbo left the Communist Party; he left Turin and went to live in Rome. And there were Calvino and Bollati, who hadn't been there very long. But they were still very young. And I had the feeling that the publishing house was losing its way. Then there had been this major break when Balbo left the Communist Party. This upset Calvino. Then Balbo left.

SINIBALDI So it was the end of a climate of solidarity, unity.

GINZBURG A climate of friendship, solidarity, and shared common goals, as well.

SINIBALDI Did you, Giulio Einaudi, have the same feeling, the same sense that things were breaking up in those years?

EINAUDI Well, I agree with her about the great loss that the publishing house lived through, the pain we all felt. But it too was a heroic period—if you think of the years '50 to '56, which marked the next real crisis in the publishing house, the goings-on in Hungary. I remember Calvino's collaboration with Vittorini, the Gettoni series.[16] The Gettoni were born out of those years. This was an authentic search for literature that brought to the fore writers who went on to become famous.

GINZBURG Yes, it's true.

EINAUDI It brought out Calvino, Bassani, Cassola.

GINZBURG Yes, yes, that's true.

EINAUDI And Bollati, you say, was young: he was young but he was already really good.

GINZBURG Absolutely.

EINAUDI And behind him was also, as general secretary, someone who became one of the greatest editors Italy has, Luciano Foà.

GINZBURG There was Luciano Foà. Yes, of course.

EINAUDI So, as I say, it was an extraordinary period. Pavese's death was a huge blow, it isn't as if we just carried on, "just picked up the baton," as the saying goes.

GINZBURG What do you mean, the baton?

SINIBALDI The baton that had fallen.

EINAUDI Others picked it up willingly, didn't they?

GINZBURG Yes, that's true.

SINIBALDI But those were also the years about which we hear these criticisms of Einaudi. The Einaudi of those days doesn't exist anymore.

EINAUDI The fact is, there was an editorial group all with different ideologies—Communists, orthodox Marxists, less orthodox Marxists, Socialists, members of Partito d'Azione . . . Let's not forget that the cultural origins of the publishing house evolved around the Partito d'Azione, starting with Leone Ginzburg, then Franco Venturi,[17] then Norberto Bobbio[18] before modestly reaching me . . . that I had a certain sympathy in the Resistance for the Communist Party, because I took part in the Garibaldi Brigades, but it was never more than a sympathy. I was never a full-fledged member, as everyone knows . . . and I always argued good naturedly with the Party, demanding that Gramsci be published in as full a version as possible. [To Natalia] Remember, there were also Paolo Serini—Catholic Communists who were at the core. But everything we published was always discussed, by everyone, in meetings. And when there was a disagreement, it went to a vote, and when the majority opposed printing a book, it didn't get printed. Let's remember that Braudel was printed against the opinion of Cantimori, the Marxist.

GINZBURG Yes, yes, of course.

SINIBALDI I'm wondering, were you aware at the time that you were involved in what was also a political operation?

EINAUDI We were aware that we were performing a cultural function that, being a serious cultural function, was also a political one.

SINIBALDI Does Natalia Ginzburg agree here?

GINZBURG Yes, of course.

SINIBALDI She was telling us about the meetings of the Communist Party cell . . .

EINAUDI You would find them in all sorts of companies.

GINZBURG Yes, I said that, too.

EINAUDI It isn't that they determined the stance of the publishing house.

SINIBALDI And so when it comes to talking about censorship, about things that you as a group decided not to publish, starting with the most publicized—the rights to Nietzsche's works.

EINAUDI That, too. We do have five works by Nietzsche in our catalog, so it's not as if we rejected him. Listen, for Nietzsche's works we had a contract to include a critical introduction by Giorgio Colli. It was a contract in which Luciano Foà had shown great interest: at that time Luciano Foà, for reasons that were largely private, I think—if there was any disagreement at the root of it, he kept it to himself—when he founded the Adelphi publishing house, he said, "I would like to take over this contract." And there's a letter of mine in which I say, "We give you these rights, on condition, however, that we publish the three most important works by Nietzsche in our Universale series."

SINIBALDI But there was a degree of diffidence, let's say, toward what was then called irrationalism?

EINAUDI But irrationalism had been explored by Pavese's series. The violet-colored series.

SINIBALDI Which, in fact, exposed itself to accusations of irrationalism.

EINAUDI The truth is I don't accept the accusation that I exercised a form of cultural hegemony . . . mind you, that's no insult.

SINIBALDI You mean, it's something you'd be proud of? No, they aren't as generous as that; they accuse you of having been an instrument of cultural hegemony.

EINAUDI An instrument, no. I reject that idea.

SINIBALDI So you accept cultural hegemony on your own account but not on others' behalf.

EINAUDI That's right.

SINIBALDI Natalia Ginzburg, what was your relationship with the politics inside the publishing house during those years? Balbo was very critical later, wasn't he? And of the publishing house as well?

GINZBURG Yes, he criticized the publishing house, too.

SINIBALDI He was the first to accuse you of being too deferential toward Marxism and the Italian Communist Party.

GINZBURG Yes, he was critical, although he stayed friendly with Giulo.

EINAUDI Yes, we were good friends. He left in '50.

GINZBURG The review *Cultura e realtà* had come out at the same time, so it was '49.

EINAUDI That was Balbo's review.

SINIBALDI And toward the end of your time at Einaudi, at the time of the receivership, [19] how did this crisis affect you, Natalia Ginzburg? Was it a personal one?

GINZBURG Me? I had returned to the publishing house after leaving it as an author—but then I came back as an author, that was in '78.

SINIBALDI And this coincided exactly with the crisis.

GINZBURG The crisis hit in '82, I think. They were dramatic times.

SINIBALDI Did you feel it also as a personal loss? Of a piece of your own history, of your own life?

GINZBURG Oh, yes, I felt it. Very much so. I was afraid that my books would all just get lost.

SINIBALDI But not only this private fear, I would think.

GINZBURG No, no, no. I was also afraid that this was the end of the history of the publishing house.

SINIBALDI In that review you wrote for the journal *Paragone* you accused Giulio Einaudi of a few omissions. The first had to do with the start of the publishing house, the second, curiously, had to do with the end. You said, "Why did you neglect to talk about that moment?"

GINZBURG That moment that was so painful for everyone. And he said, "Well, they all know about it anyway . . ."

SINIBALDI That's his defense.

EINAUDI I wasn't in a position to talk about it. I didn't think it would be good for others. She can talk about these feelings, these things, because she's a writer. There's not much to tell. These are the facts.

GINZBURG I can talk about the feelings. I was in Rome; the biggest dramas were happening in Turin. I wasn't even there. It seemed a terrible time.

SINIBALDI How did you react to the way the publishing house was being managed? I want to understand if yours was also a gut reaction . . . I mean, a violent one, when presented with the possibility that it would all disappear. The fears were a lot worse than what finally happened . . .

GINZBURG Than what happened.

SINIBALDI What did you think?

GINZBURG Well, I thought it was nobody's fault.

SINIBALDI You really thought it was nobody's fault?

GINZBURG Yes, I thought that such things can happen to a publishing house. I also wrote in that piece that publishing houses can collapse for any number of reasons, not only economic ones but also cultural ones, that one of life's moments had disappeared . . .

SINIBALDI A world.

GINZBURG A world. Something had fallen into the abyss.

SINIBALDI Giulio Einaudi, did the critical conscience of Natalia Ginzburg express itself in some way during that difficult period? Did you feel it, did it make itself felt?

EINAUDI Well, it was expressed through her silences, through her pain, and then through her hopes, because I think she started to hope that this would all get going again.

SINIBALDI The publishing house?

GINZBURG Yes, of course. Frankly, at a certain moment I wanted to leave, because I was afraid that too many people had bought it up. So I wrote a few letters to Ferrero, I remember, and we argued about it. I would say, "I think there are too many buyers," but then I ended up staying. I stayed because later there didn't seem to be so many, there were less, and . . .

SINIBALDI But did you feel like you were betraying the firm? I mean, did you resist at all? Or did you relax your guard a little, in the end?

GINZBURG It felt like I was becoming detached from . . . from my true editor.

SINIBALDI We can close here, with this statement. And also everyone knows that Natalia Ginzburg's books, including the latest one, are still being published by Einaudi, and this is in some way a form of trust.

EINAUDI Because I go on asking for your books, don't I? The last one I asked for was *Serena Cruz*—it was I who asked you for that.

GINZBURG Yes, he asked me for it, that's true. Then he forgot about it.

THREE

THE JOB OF THE WRITER

Our personal happiness or unhappiness, our "terrestrial" condition, is of great importance for the things we write. I said before that at the moment someone is writing he is miraculously driven to forget the immediate circumstances of his own life. This is certainly true. But whether we are happy or unhappy leads us to write in one way or another. When we are happy our imagination is stronger; when we are unhappy our memory works with greater vitality. Suffering makes the imagination weak and lazy; it moves, but unwillingly and heavily, with the weak movements of someone who is ill, with the weariness and caution of sick, feverish limbs; it is difficult for us to turn our eyes away from our own life and our own state, from the thirst and restlessness that pervade us. And so memories of our own past constantly crop up in the things we write, our own voice constantly echoes there, and we are unable to silence it. A particular sympathy grows up between us and the characters that we invent—that our debilitated imagination is still just able to invent—a sympathy that is tender and almost maternal, warm and damp with tears, intimately physical and stifling. We are deeply, painfully rooted in every being and thing in the world, the world that has become filled with echoes and trembling and shadows, to which we are bound by a devout and passionate pity. Then we risk foundering on a dark lake of stagnant, dead water, and dragging our mind's creations down with us, so that they are left to perish among dead rats and rotting flowers in a dark, warm whirlpool. As far as the things we write are concerned there is a danger in grief just as there is a danger in happiness, because poetic beauty is a mixture of ruthlessness, pride, irony, physical tenderness, of imagination and memory, of clarity and obscurity—and if we cannot gather all these things together we are left with something meager, unreliable, and hardly alive.[1]

MARINO SINIBALDI We open this third encounter with Natalia Ginzburg by asking her what she thinks of her writing. We have picked up here and there, in texts written by our guest, occasional allusions that act a little like slivers of self-consciousness, the self-consciousness of a storyteller. Here, in the piece that we have just listened to, taken from a text entitled "My Vocation" contained in the collection The Little Virtues, an intimate theme is touched upon: the relationship between writing and happiness, or better, between writing and feelings. There's a way of writing when one is happy, and a way of writing when one is unhappy. I imagine that this insight derives from personal experience.

NATALIA GINZBURG Yes, "My Vocation" was from '49: I think I was judging the things I had written, The Road to the City and It Happened Like This. And it seemed to me that one story had been written in a state of happiness, and the other in a state of melancholy. And I had seemed to see the dangers that come from different states of mind. I have to say that as life went on I understood that when you are more adult, a state of mind is less important to writing, in that at a certain stage in your life you have so many losses that there is always an underlying unhappiness. And therefore it influences less. You learn to write in any state of mind, and you feel more . . . I wouldn't say distant from your own life but a bit readier to dominate it.

SINIBALDI When writing you must defend yourself, you say, from happiness and pain, from overwhelming happiness and overwhelming pain. Did you succeed in this?

GINZBURG I don't think so. It Happened Like This was written in a state of profound melancholy, and then someone said to me, "If you were happier, you'd write a better book." And those words stayed in my mind, because perhaps in that book there's something overly melancholic. I came to see the book as having in some way fallen short of the mark.

SINIBALDI Let's remember that it's a book from '47, so it is linked beyond all the personal goings-on to a broader historical and social situation that was, let's face it, painful.

GINZBURG Of course; but it was straight after the war, so there was some vitality.

SINIBALDI There must have been signs of enthusiasm.

GINZBURG Yes, and of vitality, in everyone, in me, too. But in writing, I submitted to a more private sensation.

SINIBALDI And a deeper one, perhaps.

GINZBURG More particular, deeper. I remember that the title It Happened Like This was suggested by Pavese.

SINIBALDI You don't favor writers who seem to be driven by the urgency of their feelings, by an excess of happiness or by overwhelming pain. Do you dislike writers who can't detach from strong feelings, on the page?

GINZBURG I like Chekhov, who is completely detached.

SINIBALDI But you don't like, for example, the Novecento writers, expressionism, forms in which feelings burst out onto the page, sometimes in a raw state?

GINZBURG For example?

SINIBALDI Kafka, for example.

GINZBURG Kafka I like a lot.

SINIBALDI [He laughs] But the kind of writing in which sentiment is communicated directly, I mean.

GINZBURG Well, the twentieth-century writers whose work I love are, yes, Kafka; Proust, if we put him in the twentieth century—but Proust is everything, so he's one thing and the other; Elsa Morante, Svevo.

SINIBALDI Yes, Elsa Morante and Sandro Penna are writers whom you quote a lot. Do they seem to you capable of this detachment? For example, pain is a fundamental theme for both writers, but there's a kind—

GINZBURG —When Elsa Morante writes she manages to reach the tops of mountains. Pain is there, but it is completely subjugated.

SINIBALDI Completely dominated.

GINZBURG Completely. Talking to others is more important than our own personal cases. You have to get to this.

SINIBALDI And this is how you perceive it in the piece you wrote that praised Elsa Morante's History: A Novel?

GINZBURG Yes.

SINIBALDI The fact that it was a novel written for others, after years, in a century in which people write . . .

GINZBURG In which everyone acts as a mirror to his own self . . . I really admired History: A Novel, and the books that came before that one. I was the first one to read Menzogna e sortilegio (Lies and sorcery); she sent me the manuscript. I had met her in Rome, and somehow she had this extraordinary faith in me and sent me the manuscript of her book. I wasn't very important at Einaudi at the time, I had only just got there, and yet she sent it to me, then I gave it to Pavese. And I remember the extraordinary emotion this manuscript stirred in me—with things written in red, corrections with red pen. And I thought it was a wonderful book, the likes of which I could never have written. I admired her a lot, and I was also envious, because she uses the third person in her narrative, and to me this has always seemed impossible. I want detachment, but I can't write unless I use the first person.

SINIBALDI Only by saying "I" . . .

GINZBURG Either an invented I or a real I, mine (me), but always looking at things from just one angle, looking at the world from just one angle. I have never managed to climb up mountains and see everything from above. And yet this is what I aspired to: but I couldn't do it.

SINIBALDI And you saw this in Menzogna e sortilegio and then, above all, in History: A Novel.

GINZBURG Yes, in Menzogna e sortilegio, in History: A Novel, in Arturo's Island.

SINIBALDI Did you follow all the stages, for example, of Menzogna e sortilegio? There are anecdotes about Elsa Morante correcting proofs in Turin . . .

GINZBURG She had developed hives. She said that printing errors made her break out in a rash. She had a temperature! She claimed this was due to the printing errors and how much they upset her. Yes, that was a happy time. She had also become friends with Pavese and Calvino . . . everyone used to meet in a certain café in Turin called Caffè Platti, which was very close to the publishing house, and she was friendly with everyone. She was happy then, in spite of the printing errors.

SINIBALDI Today we will be talking about your plays. Elsa Morante wasn't gentle, for example, with your first plays.

GINZBURG No! She didn't like them at all, neither the early ones nor any that came after.

SINIBALDI She was very open in her criticism, wasn't she?

GINZBURG Yes; she took me to dinner one evening with Adriana Asti, and she said to me—I had written *I Married You for the Fun of It*—and she said to me that she didn't like it at all, that it was fatuous, sugary. She really didn't like it; and she shouted at me. She didn't just make comments, she actually got angry. She said, "How could you do a thing like this . . . ?"

MIRELLA FULVI There was an opening gambit of hers that particularly frightened you . . .

GINZBURG "I'll tell you the truth . . ." [*She laughs*] Yes, she would say, "I'll tell you the truth," and then she would say awful things. And I would come home very downhearted, but when she reproached you, there was also something in her reproach that stimulated you, made you want to get on and work. I think that, in fact, when you write, these harsh criticisms are useful.

SINIBALDI You have a theory about the need to have people to talk to, advisors, critics who somehow offer protection to your creative activity . . .

GINZBURG Yes. But for me Elsa wasn't someone to talk to because I never got to say what I was thinking. I admired her so much, but I never got to voice my real thoughts.

SINIBALDI But is this possible among writers? You earlier made a fleeting reference to a term that can go unnoticed because it is so obvious, that of "envy."

GINZBURG Yes, but not envy of the base kind.

SINIBALDI More a kind of admiration.

GINZBURG Yes, the admiration of someone who would like to be able to do something vaguely similar but can't. So it wasn't some low kind of envy . . . it wasn't a sense of demeaning aversion toward someone who does something that is better.

SINIBALDI No, otherwise you wouldn't talk about her in this way. Do you have a theory of your own about literature?

GINZBURG No, I haven't.

SINIBALDI But an idea about your job of writing about yourself. Listen to this extract:

And you have to realize that you cannot hope to console yourself for your grief by writing. You cannot deceive yourself by hoping for caresses and lullabies from your vocation. In my life there have been interminable, desolate empty Sundays in which I desperately wanted to write something that would console me for my loneliness and boredom, so that I could be calmed and soothed by phrases and words. But I could not write a single line. My vocation has always rejected me, it does not want to know about me. Because this vocation is never a consolation or a way of passing the time. It is not a companion. This vocation is a master who is able to beat us till the blood flows, a master who reviles and condemns us. We must swallow our saliva and tears and grit our teeth and dry the blood from our wounds and serve him. Serve him when he asks. Then he will help us up onto our feet, fix our feet firmly on the ground; he will help us overcome madness and delirium, fever and despair. But he has to be the one who gives the orders, and he always refuses to pay attention to us when we need him.

GINZBURG Elsa Morante didn't like this piece, and she didn't like the fact that I titled it *Il mio mestiere*.[2] She said writing wasn't a job. "Mestiere" was a word that she rejected. She wasn't keen on my essays as a whole, whereas she did like my novels.

SINIBALDI Because the word "mestiere" seemed too prosaic a concept?

GINZBURG I don't know, she didn't agree with it, she said it wasn't the right word. But I left it, it was the first word I had found and I had grown to like it.

FULVI You said just now that Elsa Morante's criticisms could be harsh, and yet in them you found a kind of recognition.

GINZBURG Yes, of course. There was a generosity about these criticisms, there was profound attention given, which in some way gave new breath, space, the desire to carry on. And when you're writing, there's nothing worse than that drizzly indifference, that drizzly desire to please that you see in people who don't really care.

FULVI Have you met that?

GINZBURG Yes, endlessly, we meet it all the time. And that gives you a sense of discouragement, of futility, of superfluousness in everything you can do.

SINIBALDI It occurred to me that these observations on literature would be useful to young or aspiring writers. Because they contain a strong, severe idea of this job—I must say this term seems to me to be . . .

GINZBURG Fair.

SINIBALDI Yes, absolutely fair, and one that has to do with an almost ethical vision of this profession, implying also commitment, dedication, and not only talent and vocation. The fact is, you read many manuscripts over the years, I think especially during those last years at Einaudi. What impression do you have of that writing? Not only of the texts that you published—because you pushed for the publication of some of the younger writers or the new writers (if that is how to call them, or at least, those that you loved). But in general, what impression did you get from your reading? Did you have, for example, the sensation—to use that very useful reproach that was made toward you so many years ago by Carlo Levi—that people were writing by chance, that there was a lack of motivation—that there was a lack of motivation in so many of these literary débuts?

GINZBURG I've had the impression that some of the manuscripts I read were written by people who . . . who had never really read. They were writing without reading. And there was something flabby about their writing, or else there was something too literary, too rigid; and there were these two paths people took, it seems to me. But then when reading manuscripts I can sometimes make terrible blunders: I don't want to name these blunders now [*she laughs*] but I do make them, that is, I take a fancy to things that then perhaps my son will read and say, "This is awful!"

SINIBALDI [*He laughs*] Just your son? That surely isn't so important.

GINZBURG Well, then, perhaps Einaudi rejects the ones I've chosen. But then there are also sometimes manuscripts about which I'm sure, but they don't let them through. But I am sure so I want to go on fighting for them. And this sometimes pays off.

SINIBALDI You sometimes win, get your own way? This tells us something about how publishing works, then . . .

GINZBURG Well, only sometimes: for example, the book by Alice Ceresa I liked enormously: *Bambine* (Little girls). They were a bit diffident, there was a lot of "um-ing" and "ah-ing." And yet it's a lovely book, and it's had some really serious reviews. I heard it had sold out, and it is in my opinion a lovely book. I didn't like much the one before it, *La figlia prodiga* (Prodigal daughter), I couldn't get into that.

But this one, on the other hand, really got to me, and I asked them to publish it, and then they did. But sometimes I fight for . . .

SINIBALDI For lost causes.

GINZBURG Yes, for books that I can't get them to publish.

SINIBALDI Do special relationships develop between you and authors?

GINZBURG When I was an established consultant at Einaudi (now I'm not a consultant, I'm not anything) I worked full-time. And I wrote letters, quite long ones, and authors would reply. I would sign them "Giulio Einaudi, Editor," but then every now and then . . . at a certain point they found out that it must be me, so then they would write to me. Yes, I had some quite protracted correspondences.

SINIBALDI Did you like this work, this kind of production . . . of literary production?

GINZBURG Yes, I liked it.

SINIBALDI Didn't you sometimes want to get away from this editorial responsibility, for example, as regards a young writer? Does this aspect of the work appeal to you?

GINZBURG No, now I'm getting so many manuscripts arriving at my house, I've got a huge pile of them. I can never find the time, I feel I owe a lot of reading time.

SINIBALDI Well, let's say this publicly so . . .

GINZBURG Yes. In that way they won't get anxious!

SINIBALDI . . . so naturally they won't expect replies.

GINZBURG It's hard. When can you find the time to read all these manuscripts?

SINIBALDI Of course.

GINZBURG Either I can't find the time or I just want to have a bit of time to myself and do nothing. Sometimes I just don't want to read manuscripts.

SINIBALDI You won the Viareggio Prize in '57, I think.

GINZBURG Yes.

SINIBALDI With a short novel entitled *Valentino*. It's a story with a new twist to it because of the male character you created for it. Do you remember . . . ?

GINZBURG Of course.

SINIBALDI It really struck me, because it offers the first positive portrait of a homosexual, I think, in Italian literature—it came just before Bassani's *The Gold-Rimmed Spectacles*.

GINZBURG Yes.

SINIBALDI It was part of a new way of feeling; you would bring out again these inept, rather amorphous male figures that had been such an intrinsic part of your earlier writing, only this time they were written about in a way that was richer, so much more alive—do you agree? Were you aware of this male figure who was growing inside you?

GINZBURG Yes, yes, of course. I had in mind a physical person but one who wasn't at all homosexual. And the homosexuality I discovered while I was writing the story: I knew there was something hidden, but I didn't know what. And it just came to me one day . . . He was homosexual! And so then the relationship he had with that friend who then kills himself came out, and the whole story unraveled, just like that . . .

SINIBALDI Unraveled, or grew? "Unraveled" seems a bit of a negative term, perhaps . . . [He laughs]

GINZBURG Ah, yes. But when I began the story, I didn't know how it would end. I knew that there was a house . . .

SINIBALDI You didn't know what Valentino was like, just as the reader didn't?

GINZBURG No, I knew that there was a house, I was thinking vaguely of Turin (I was in Turin); then I knew . . . I knew four things: I knew how this Valentino was made, that he tried clothes on in front of the mirror, he tried on wind-breakers, sportswear, he played with the kitten, and that there was something secret about him. And then at a certain point I had a flash—Oh, he was homosexual!

SINIBALDI A revelation.

GINZBURG Yes.

SINIBALDI And these were the years in which you were getting closer to "autobiography." You once wrote, "I have crept toward autobiography stealthily like a wolf." And in fact, it wasn't very fast.

GINZBURG *Valentino* is a story that is totally made up; but I had taken two or three faces from real life. Physical faces. There was that; the rest was entirely made up. And then I wrote *Sagittario* in that same period, which was again a made-up story—where there was a mother, some daughters. Made-up. Then . . . then in England I wrote *Voices in the Evening*.

SINIBALDI *Voices in the Evening.* Right, so now we're in the sixties—that came out in '61.

GINZBURG Yes. I wrote it in twenty days. At the time there didn't seem to be anything autobiographical in it, but I was wrong, because in fact I had put Ivrea in it, perhaps one of my brothers.

SINIBALDI Not your own family as such: at this stage of getting closer you went through your family's "neighbors"—we will see in a moment what kind of neighbors there are in *Voices in the Evening*.

GINZBURG Yes, they were changed, but a bit of them was there.

SINIBALDI People from your real life. You were in England: can you tell us how you ended up in England?

GINZBURG I had gone with Gabriele.

SINIBALDI Gabriele Bandini, your second husband, an Anglicist.

GINZBURG He had been nominated for three consecutive years as director of the Italian Cultural Institute. And I went with him. I never managed to get on with English, and I didn't learn it.

SINIBALDI This is the main negative result, then, of your stay in England.

GINZBURG I couldn't do it. He spoke English perfectly. They mistook him for an Englishman, whereas I . . . I didn't.

SINIBALDI But they didn't mistake you for an Englishwoman.

GINZBURG Gosh, I could hardly say a word! I had learned to say, "Have a cigarette?" When people came over—"Have a drink?" Then those three or four things you say—

SINIBALDI —for daily survival.

GINZBURG Yes, but I couldn't understand when they replied. And . . . and then . . . well, I missed Italy so badly.

SINIBALDI But did you think of your father? One of your father's ideals, one of his idols, was England, I think, so I learned from *The Things We Used to Say*: England, Socialism.

GINZBURG Yes, but I was against my father's idols!

[*Laughter*]

FULVI Including learning languages well . . .

GINZBURG Learning languages well. With English, I don't know why, they made me study it, but I never learned it. And yet I read Ivy Compton-Burnett in English. Perhaps I knew it a bit more . . .

SINIBALDI You didn't want to admit you knew it?

GINZBURG No . . . yes, but Gabriele bought me all of Ivy Compton-Burnett's books, because he wanted me to learn English a little—but I just couldn't. And so I read almost all of the books by this writer whom I really love; and they're books that are almost all dialogue. And

I started writing *Voices in the Evening* with this dialogic way of writing in my head. And I remember I was really happy writing all these dialogues. To be constantly starting a new line felt like I was doing something totally new.

SINIBALDI In *Voices in the Evening*, memory starts to intervene in some way even at the drawing board stage. You wrote that you were thinking of doing a short story two or three pages long. Then out of nowhere, with no prior thought, into the story came the places of your childhood: Turin, the streets, the countryside.

GINZBURG Yes, Turin and Ivrea.

SINIBALDI Which you didn't love.

GINZBURG That's true, but for which I suddenly felt a nostalgia. And I think that creativity is born out of nostalgia: because even when I wrote *The Road to the City*, I was nostalgic for Turin, and I was mixing it with . . .

SINIBALDI With the Abruzzi, with exile.

GINZBURG With the Abruzzi. And there, I was nostalgic for Italy, and I had recreated . . .

SINIBALDI A not wholly imaginary Italy, rather a semireal one, and that was the discovery . . .

93

GINZBURG Semireal: and yet very far from me at that time, people who were very far.

SINIBALDI So, *Voices in the Evening* is the story of the failure of love during the decline of an industrial dynasty . . .

GINZBURG There isn't much of the industrial, though.

SINIBALDI But you understand that it is the story of an industrial dynasty.

GINZBURG Yes.

SINIBALDI Let's listen to an extract, the one in which the end of this love is declared.

The next morning I got up and dressed very quietly, without letting my mother hear me; and I went to the Casa Tonda.

I had never been there alone. I had been there, of course, with my mother, with Gemmina, or often with Raffaella.

Tommasino came to open the door for me. He was already up and dressed, although it was early; and he had put on a thick gray shaggy pullover, although outside a hot sunny day was beginning.

"Salve," he said to me without showing any surprise. "I am unwell, I've caught a cold; I probably had a bit of a temperature last night. That is why I have put on this pullover."

There he was in the dining room, with his pullover drawn down over his thin body, and the cuffs full of handkerchiefs.

He had a small sponge in his hand and was cleaning his tape recorder.

"Do you want to say something into the tape recorder?" he said. "Hearing one's own voice is interesting. To begin with, I could not bear it; I found my voice horrid, a falsetto voice. Then I got accustomed to it. But it is interesting. Try it."

I said, "No."

I had sat down. I had my hands in my jacket pockets, and I looked at him. I looked at him, I looked at his head, his ruffled hair, his long big pullover, his thin hands that could not keep still and made continuous gestures.

"I have come to return the ring to you," I said.

And I drew it out of my pocket; it was small with a small pearl; this ring that he had given to me had belonged to his mother, Signora Cecilia.

He took it and laid it on the table.

"You don't want to marry me," he said.

"No," I said. "How can you think that I still want to marry you after the things that you said to me yesterday?"

"Yesterday," he said, "I was depressed, taking a gloomy view of things. I probably felt that I was going to have a temperature."

"However, of course," he said, "you are right; it is better so." I gazed round, and said,

"I have pictured everything only too clearly. I have pictured you and me, here, in this room, in this house. I have pictured everything with great exactness down to the smallest details. And when one sees the things of the future so clearly as though they were already happening, it is a sign that they should never happen. They have already happened in a sense in our minds, and it is really not possible to experience them further."

I said, "It is like, on some days, the air is too clear, too transparent, and one sees everything sharply and exactly outlined, and then one will say that rain is coming."

"How calm you are!" he said. "You do not cry; you say everything so calmly."

"And I?" he said. "What shall I do?"

"You will do as you have always done," I said.

"And you?" he said. "What will you do?"

"I, too, shall do as I have always done," I said.

"How calm we are!" he said. "How cool, quiet, calm!

"I hope," he said, twisting his hair round his fingers, "that you may some day meet a man better than me.

"You see, it is not in me," he said, "no real vitality. This is my great want. I feel a shudder of disgust when I should assert myself. I want to assert myself, and then I have this shudder. Anybody else, with a shudder like that—well, he does not take any account of it, he puts it out of his mind at once. But I keep it in my mind for a long time.

"It is because I have the feeling," he said, "that they have already lived enough, those others before me that they have already consumed all the reserves, all the vitality that there was for us. The others, Nebbia, Vincenzino, my father. Nothing was left over for me.

"The others," he said, "all those who have lived in this village before me. It seems to me that I am only their shadow."

He said, "In earlier days, after Vincenzino died, I thought that I should have realized all his plans. He had heaps of them ready, designs for the factory, canteens, restrooms, quarters for the workers. They were sensible, practicable things, not just dreams. He never had time to bring them to completion. I thought that I should do that myself.

"Instead," he said, "I have been no good at doing anything. I always say 'yes' to Purillo. I don't have the will to hold out against him, to contest. I knuckle under and say 'yes.'"

"Sometimes," he said, "I have an idea of going away from this place. To find a bit of vitality."

"I shall go to Canada perhaps," he said. "Some time ago, last year, Borzaghi told me he could get me some work there, in Canada, in Montreal."

"Canada," I said. "I don't know what it is like. I imagine it must be a place full of wood."

"Yes," he said, and smiled, "there must be quite a bit of wood there. Forests."

One could see the Villa Rondine from the windows, one could see Purillo playing tennis in the garden with Borzaghi's son.

"Look at him there," said Tommasino, gazing through the panes. "Look at him there—Purillo, fine fellow. Now, he has got plenty of vitality or, rather, he has not so much got it as that he behaves as if he had, and he gets the results he wants."

"Perhaps it is just because he is stupid," he said, "and he has never realized they have already exhausted all the vitality that was available in this place.

"How a place can get one down!" he said. "It has a weight of lead, with all its dead. This village of ours, it just gets me down; it is so small, a handful of houses. I can never free myself from it, I cannot forget it. Even if I end up in Canada, I shall take it with me!

"If only you had been a girl," he said, "from another village! If only I had found you in Montreal or somewhere, if only we had met there and married! We should have felt so free, so unburdened, without these houses, these hills, these mountains. Free as a bird, I should have been!

"But even if I took you with me to Montreal now," he said, "it would be just like it is here; we should not be able to create anything new. We should probably still go on talking about Vincenzino and Nebbia and Purillo. It would be exactly the same as being here.

"After all, I wonder whether I shall ever go there, to Montreal," he said.

"And now you must go along," he said, and he took my face between his hands. "You must go, like this, without crying, without shedding even a single tear. Go along with dry eyes, quite open and calm. It is not worthwhile to shed tears, and I want to remember you like that."

"Ciao, good-bye, Elsa," he said, and I said, "Ciao, good-bye, Tommasino." And I came away.[3]

SINIBALDI With *Voices in the Evening*, we come close to autobiography: you wrote that you were even happy to be able to mention surnames; previously you had found the practice repugnant.

GINZBURG I had never dared use surnames, for a very simple and personal reason: all the surnames that came into my head were Jewish ones, and I didn't want them all to be Jewish. I wanted to be mixed in with everyone.

SINIBALDI But obviously there was a good reason you only thought of Jewish surnames.

GINZBURG Yes . . . and finally in *The Things We Used to Say* I used Jewish surnames, real ones.

SINIBALDI Beyond the transparent one, so to speak, of De Francisci, we see another surname, that of the Olivetti family.

GINZBURG Well, maybe, yes.

SINIBALDI The industrial dynasty, so to speak, close to your family.

GINZBURG Yes . . . it isn't their story and it isn't that they are really these characters. But I imagined a family rather like the Olivettis as I knew them. I think that Vincenzino, who is the dead brother of Tommasino, was based a little on Adriano.

SINIBALDI Adriano Olivetti, with this burning desire for reform, for things to change.

GINZBURG A little, yes.

SINIBALDI Adriano Olivetti married your sister. How do you judge the political adventures of Adriano Olivetti? The main one was the "Community" movement, an attempt to create industrial reform from above, with forms of co-management, with advanced assistance for the workers. So, a really huge and somewhat utopian scheme.

GINZBURG Well, it seems to me now that he was right about many things: I think that his idea of communities was a good one, a fair one. Perhaps it was out of its time, I don't know. He was a very strange person: at home my family was hugely fond of him. My father was very fond of him, but he said Adriano was crazy, and so did my mother. They found him a bit crazy: my father was materialistic, whereas Adriano, well, he would turn to wizards for health cures. So, it was all a . . .

SINIBALDI A consistent cultural gap.

GINZBURG Very much so, yes. But for all that, they never argued; but my father, yes, he thought Adriano was a bit mad. A bit before 25 July he was arrested because he had some kind of relationship, I couldn't say what, with María José.

SINIBALDI With the attempts to turn everything upside down starting from the top levels of Fascism, as it were.

GINZBURG Yes, exactly. He was in prison, and he was in prison even after 25 July. They didn't let him out straightaway. Then I met him in Rome that October. And when Leone was arrested, Adriano came to get me and saved us, I think. He took us to a convent because the

Germans could come at any moment. He was an extremely coura-
geous man, an extraordinary man. He was a strange mixture of en-
gineer and . . . with something prophetic about him.

SINIBALDI Your brother, Gino Martinoli, worked directly with Olivetti. Olivetti even became a member of Parliament in '58, not long
before his death in 1960. He had developed an idea of direct political
intervention. Not an experience that interested you?

GINZBURG Not much, no, not at that time. But later on I thought
that perhaps his idea of communities was a fair one. But it didn't
have much success.

SINIBALDI It is one of the many failed inspirations of the Italian
Novecento, full of maestros with no followers.

GINZBURG Well, he *was* a strange man. Once, so I was told, he was
going to the factory and had no umbrella, and he got soaked in the
rain, and so he ordered who knows how many umbrellas so that the
workers who had forgotten their umbrellas could have one.

SINIBALDI A fine example of concrete social reform.

GINZBURG Yes. He was extremely generous. He was forever handing
out money; he was very generous to me when I was an internee.

SINIBALDI The chapter of a book dedicated to Natalia Ginzburg starts
like this, with a phrase that is perhaps even ironic: "After cultivating
for years a 'sacred horror of autobiography,' Ginzburg writes in 1962
The Things We Used to Say." After rejecting autobiography, the pathetic,
the sentimentality often found in memories that come directly from
childhood and from one's own family, Ginzburg writes a novel that
comes in the guise of an autobiography, *The Things We Used to Say*.[4]

GINZBURG Which I don't think is sentimental: I didn't want to make
a sentimental book. I didn't want to write about my own experience
of childhood. I wanted to write about my family and talk more about
them than about myself. In the end I came into it as well, but . . .

SINIBALDI The least present person in the book is you.

GINZBURG I had no desire to tell what I felt as a child, really, I didn't
want to. When I was small, I would think, "I would like to write a
book with all these people in it and all the things they say," when I
looked at them. When I was very small, about eight, I had written
a play, where they came in and went out, said things that they always said. There was my brother Alberto who said, "Mom, give me
two lire!" and the jokes they made all the time. And this dialogue—I
had called it *Dialogue*—this dialogue was read by the family, and they

would laugh; they really liked it, they said it was sweet. And I wanted to write about living in that time.

SINIBALDI So it was a very long time gestating inside you, we now find out.

GINZBURG Very long, yes.

SINIBALDI In '63 *The Things We Used to Say* won the Strega Prize and was enormously successful.

GINZBURG Yes, it was the first book of mine to be successful, because the ones before it weren't. Einaudi printed them, they printed three thousand copies, then maybe they did a reprint, but they weren't highly successful.

SINIBALDI They were confined to a small market, but here you reached the wider public. I saw in *Corriere della Sera* from July of that same year a photo of you with the editor Einaudi and underneath an enthusiastic, glowing, even embarrassing caption, "Woman of the Day." How did you deal with this sudden success?

GINZBURG Well, I had won the Strega Prize, and there were other people who clearly deserved it. So I did get a sense that I had won something that I didn't deserve, because in that year there was Landolfi and there was Primo Levi with *The Truce*. But still, mine was a book that was successful, people still read it today. The thing that surprised me the most was that children read it. I really didn't expect that.

SINIBALDI Because you had thought of your peers as your audience, people who could understand what went on . . . the background?

GINZBURG Yes.

SINIBALDI There is an explanation for its success, and it's in something you once said. You said, "I don't know if it is my best book, but it is certainly the only book I wrote in a state of absolute freedom."

GINZBURG That's true. For one thing, I was using Jewish surnames. I was doing dialogue or not doing dialogue, it didn't matter: I didn't have the constrictions of the imagination. I was throwing away everything that could have been invented, I would think of something and say, "No, I'm making that up." I was looking for the truth, what I remembered. It's a book that comes straight from my memory.

SINIBALDI The thing that holds this memory together—any reader knows it, and will have been struck by it—is just this way of expressing things. A theorist of modern literature might call it "a system of signs." That is, a system of words, a network of words, ways of speaking, slogans, phrases, verbal tics . . .

99

GINZBURG Yes, things people said at home.

SINIBALDI Insults: "half-wits" and "dagoes" for insults; "muddles," "mucks," "messes": these words became indelibly fixed in your memory.

GINZBURG Yes, of course: they were the words my father used.

FULVI So I'm curious to know: how did your family react when The Things We Used to Say came out? We know, because Gino Martinoli himself told us, that he believes your book was very truthful. But we know that not everyone in the family agreed about this.

GINZBURG Well . . . my sister got angry. She said that my parents were not like that, that they were much, much better, that it was a gossipy, stupid book. She got very angry. Others . . . no.

FULVI Your father?

GINZBURG My father at first was very worried. He said, "I don't want Natalia to write a book that will throw mud at our family." But then when he read it, it seems as if he enjoyed it—he was laughing. And my mother was already dead.

SINIBALDI Let's listen to an extract from The Things We Used to Say; we'd like Natalia Ginzburg to read a piece she has chosen.

GINZBURG Well, it's a little piece from the end. It's my father and mother talking to each other, and my father says:

"Poor Cesare, my brother, was too fat. He used to eat too much. I don't want Alberto, who eats so much, getting as fat as poor Cesare."

"Everybody ate too much. People ate too much in those days. I remember Grandmother Dolcetta, how much she ate."

"On the other hand my mamma, poor soul, ate very little. She was slim. My mamma was a great beauty when she was young, poor soul. She had a beautiful head of hair. Everyone said she had a beautiful head of hair. She used to give lunch parties for fifty or sixty guests as well. There would be ices with hot sauces and ices with cold. They ate very well."

"My cousin Regina looked so elegant at those lunches. She was a real beauty, Regina, a really beautiful woman."

"Oh no, Beppino," said my mother, "she was a sham beauty."

"Ah, you're wrong there, she was really beautiful. I was so fond of her. Poor Cesare was fond of her too. But when she was young she was a bit of a flirt. She was a terrible flirt. Even my mamma always said that Regina was a terrible flirt."

"My uncle the Daftie sometimes used to go to your mamma's lunch parties," my mother said.

"Sometimes. Not always, though. Daftie used to put on airs a bit; he thought they were a rather bourgeois and reactionary set. He put on airs a bit, your uncle."

"He was such a nice man," my mother said. "He was so nice, Daftie, so witty. He was like Silvio. Silvio took after him."

"My dear Signor Lipmann," said my mother. "Do you remember how he used to say that? And he always used to say, 'Blessed are the orphans.' He used to say that a lot of lunatics go mad because of their parents. Blessed are the orphans, he always used to say. He had got to the bottom of psychoanalysis when it hadn't even been invented yet."

"My dear Signor Lipmann," said my mother. "I feel as if I can hear him saying it now."

"My mamma kept a carriage, poor soul," said my father. "She used to go for a drive in her carriage every day."

"She always used to take Gino and Mario in the carriage with her," said my mother. "And after a bit they would start being sick because the smell of leather upset them and they would dirty the whole carriage, and she would be so cross."

"Poor soul," said my father. "She was so upset when she had to give up her carriage."

"Pour soul," said my father. "When I came back from Spitzberg, where I went into the cranium of a whale to look for the cerebro-spinal ganglia, I had my clothes with me in a bag, all filthy with the whale's blood, and she was too disgusted to touch them. I put them in the attic, and they stank the house out."

"I didn't manage to find the cerebro-spinal ganglia," said my father. "My mamma kept saying, 'He's ruined those good clothes for nothing.'"

"Perhaps you didn't look for them properly, Beppino," said my mother. "Perhaps you should have had another try."

"Bah! You're nothing but a half-wit! It wasn't exactly a simple matter, you know! You're always trying to put me down. You're such a donkey!"

"When I was at boarding school," said my mother, "they taught me about whales, too. They were good at teaching natural history. I really enjoyed it. But they used to take us to Mass a bit too often at my boarding school. We were always having to go to confession.

Sometimes we couldn't think of a sin to confess, so we would say, 'I stole some snow.' 'I stole some snow.' Oh, it was such fun at my boarding school. I did enjoy it."

"On Sundays," she said, "I used to go to see Walrus. They called Walrus's sisters the 'Saintlies' because they were terribly pious. Walrus's real name was Perego. His friends made up a poem about him:

> Morning and evening a pleasure to view
> Is Perego's house and his wine cellar, too."

"Oh we're not going to start on Walrus now, are we?" said my father. "How many times have I heard that story!"

SINIBALDI Eugenio Montale identified one of the characteristics of this book as the "continuous bass of gossip," the idle chatter, the rattling on almost without purpose. These exchanges produce a sense of estrangement, they stop revealing anything, they are pure communication.

GINZBURG Yes, of course; but then after I found that I couldn't use the word "I" anymore, because it seemed to me that "I" meant "I" as in the one from *The Things We Used to Say*. And so this word "I," which I had used so much, inventing different people, I couldn't use anymore in novels, and this made me anxious.

SINIBALDI How did you get over this problem? In the novels that followed, this word "I" would be avoided, almost abandoned, it seems.

GINZBURG Avoided.

SINIBALDI Let's listen to Montale:

When Natalia Ginzburg was still a young writer . . . Silvio Benco said of her prose that you were constantly aware of the "pulse of truth"—but, beware, nothing more than a pulse. After her early books, this character, partly to do with style but mainly dictated by a whole way of understanding and communicating reality, became more and more established until it reached perhaps its best expression in the short novel *Voices in the Evening*. From then on, having tuned her instrument to perfection, Ginzburg had only to stay faithful to a subject that was totally fitting to her simple vocality. I would say that every page of Ginzburg is instantly recognizable for its delicacy and for a touch so light it is almost insignificant, for her capacity to imitate not so much the voice of whoever is talking so much as the cadenza of his chatter.

This technique was more fitting than ever for that "outline" of her family life, which Natalia has entitled *The Things We Used to Say*, not forgetting to highlight the fact that in the Levi family the use of our language must have been anything but orthodox. If every family group has its own unique language, you can believe that in the house of Professor Giuseppe Levi (called the "Tomato," perhaps because his hair had a tinge of red) the family's language was one of the affectionate ties of that group. Either way, the language in *The Things We Used To Say* is, in fact, below the average level of our "standard" of conversation. It is a savvy way of talking that stays firmly on the ground and gains in immediacy what it would lose if it were to invest in a subject with more dimension, in which the flowing nature of time was allowed to play its part. But not for nothing does time remain the great absent entity in the present tale. The narration, which covers at least forty years—pre-Fascism, Fascism and post-Fascism seen from a strictly personal vantage point, almost as if it were a children's story rather than a burning memory—reduces everything to the smallest denominator of a gesture that has stuck in the memory, the color of a look or a dress, stripping everything (men and things) of its gravity until it becomes almost unreal. The world has no weight for Natalia, who admits to being bored by and incompetent at music, painting, and everything other than poetry and, above all, admits to being incapable of living a life that is not in poetry.

Half-asleep, seemingly absent, Natalia manages with few words to outline characters whom we have known and loved; but she reduces them all to the same proportions. Everything counts, nothing counts to Natalia outside of the lazy sweetness of allowing herself to live . . .

Perhaps there is something cruel in Natalia's art, the desire to be gently cruel in the way that only a woman can. But cruel with a certain languor, with the semblance of semi-irresponsibility. When all is said and done, in her, on the surface, gentleness prevails; and this explains why her art is as pleasing to men as to women. The day Natalia gives us something that is all for men, some of her equilibrium will have been lost. I'm not sure if that would be an entirely bad thing, and I'm not sure, either, whether we should wish for that day to come, so singular does this art of hers seem to be, even in the places where, as in *The Things We Used to Say*, the unadorned but conscious negligence in depiction hints at the danger of mannerism.[5]

SINIBALDI I have the impression that underneath the concessions—he liked the book—he had, all the same, some strong reservations. Is that true?

GINZBURG Well, because one of these "loved characters" was my Aunt Drusilla, the Fly.[6]

SINIBALDI The Fly, Montale's muse . . .

GINZBURG Yes, he thought I had made her into a caricature, when instead she was very important to him. In fact, I didn't make a true portrait of the Fly; it was as I saw her as a child, this Aunt Drusilla who . . .

SINIBALDI More a sketch than a portrait.

GINZBURG Yes, yes.

FULVI Who "had her little bits and pieces"?

GINZBURG Who "had her little bits and pieces," who said, "Has Andrea also got his little bits and pieces?" Then she would have her milk brought to her earlier, and would say, "I'm happy to pay just a bit more, but bring me my milk first!" But they just took it to her at the same time as everyone else!

SINIBALDI There's a little phrase, a short comment that Montale makes—"The world has no weight for Natalia." It seems strange, it seems as if you think that we must pretend the world has no weight.

GINZBURG It is very weighty.

SINIBALDI In order to write we must pretend it has no weight, just as we must separate ourselves from pain.

GINZBURG Yes, of course; but it does have its own enormous weight. I have a world that is certainly incomplete, because I lack a cultural background. So when I write I pick up little pieces, the pieces that I can find, but I have this limitation.

SINIBALDI But do you believe that a cultural background is really necessary to someone who writes?

GINZBURG I don't know, I've got it into my head that what I'm really lacking is a cultural background.

SINIBALDI This is an idea that we will not try to contest, given that you so often repeat it. [*He laughs*]

GINZBURG Yes, because it is a thing that I feel. I always believed that . . . the more experienced I became, the more I would gain of this background. But it isn't so.

SINIBALDI Another reviewer was Giansiro Ferrata. Let's hear what he says.

Ginzburg in *The Things We Used to Say* has almost always managed to find the exact balance: on the one hand offering us a kind of re-covered or, rather, reawakened adolescence, with its inexhaustible hints of malice, the easy flow of memories, the feelings untainted even by later resentment and, on the other, a practical maturity associated with suffering, limitations to her youthful horizons, and new forms of reality. After the abuse that was made of "memory literature" in the period 1930–1940, it is still really hard to give it back its energy. Ginzburg has succeeded by following a method that she takes directly from her essays, clinging to "real things"; but with how much freshness in her skill, and how much commit-ment to a meaning that is both moral and poetic. The details were bound to be many, given the sense of reconstruction of an entire development of a reality and its various associations—sentimental, reflective, and habitual. Even if not all of these details are in focus, the narrative never falls into the picturesque tones of an old picture or into the easy anecdote created for external consumption: every page tends to characterize with a lightness of touch (but delving deeply) a system of human relationships that change and attempts to hold them still, not to let them change, attempts to which only memory can give any lasting support.

To have created a story, an essentially "private" one, with a clar-ity that is both simple and modern, and against a rational back-ground, making it a kind of affectionate but not indulgent public trial of a family's life and relationships, to have done this today is the sign of a unique kind of courage that is not brazen but just productive in the frankest way possible. . . . [7]

SINIBALDI That allusion to an adolescent, childlike way of seeing things is interesting. As you know, this is a cliché of a certain kind of literature of the twentieth century: the need for, the love of an ado-lescent look on life. I think this could be said of Elsa Morante, Sandro Penna, Saba, and Pascoli who is so important in understanding your early, childhood reading. Have you thought of this, this adolescent view, as a way of rediscovering the world?

GINZBURG I thought that I must try to tell it as I saw it then, not with the thoughts that I could have had after, but as I saw it then. But I knew that I didn't want to present myself as a child, I didn't want that; that is, without my childhood feelings, I could write a book about my childhood feelings . . .

SINIBALDI . . . which are not featured at all in *The Things We Used to Say.*

GINZBURG They're not featured. It's all just through the eyes . . .

SINIBALDI Yes, in fact, it is exactly the point at which a child's eyes . . .

GINZBURG Eyes and ears. Yes.

SINIBALDI . . . and the senses, of course. A child's senses. And it was this that Ferrata picked up on, when he said that you had adopted a childlike view . . .

GINZBURG I think so. Anyhow, that is what I wanted to do: not to be there myself, but to look at them and listen to them.

SINIBALDI We can't leave out the opinion of Cesare Garboli, whose opinion, we know, is always important to you, and is often definitive, whether in good or bad terms:

There is, in Ginzburg's writing, and you see it also in *The Things We Used to Say*, an obscure, insolvable contradiction; a wave of thoughts that breaks continuously over another. According to Ginzburg, poetic feeling is the privilege of children (that is, in this context, metaphorical children); thanks to a personal and, in this case, feminine variant, Ginzburg too brings a good pinch of incense to burn in the tripod of the poetics of the "little child." But there is in Ginzburg also the awareness of a mysterious dialectic, of a tension between two moral opposites: yes, you can't be a poet without being a child. The eyes of poetry are the eyes of childhood. But the opposite law is also true: that is, you can only be a poet if you suffer from a longing that is never satisfied, a desperate need to be adult, to become parents. If there is a message in Ginzburg's work, it is to be found in the courage with which the writer accepts the whole weight of the alternative, placing herself in a difficult balance that offers nothing but conflict. Narrative or essay, Ginzburg's interest focuses always on the point at which adult life is at stake, hanging in the balance, because it is deprived of a pair of eyes that can see it with justice and mercy from a hazy distance, looking both from below and from above. In this way the writer avoids giving any relief to the tale and kills all perspective. Like the eyes of a child, so too the eyes of God are not bound to distinguish between futile and important things: everything is important. [8]

SINIBALDI I think that this extract of Garboli's confirms and completes what we were saying: this double optic, he calls it, of parent and child, that is, an adolescent viewpoint but mingled with memory from later years. And the other element in all of this is the feminine point of view, a factor that Garboli seems to highlight often in you, even going as far as to see in it elements of a trauma, the trauma of woman who encounters the world, of the woman who encounters the man, "the male," is that so? this is somewhat of an "idée fixe."

GINZBURG Yes.

SINIBALDI How do you react to this interpretation by Garboli?

GINZBURG Well, there is truth in it in that I had all these brothers and my childhood world was a world in which a child was alone in the middle of all these adults.

SINIBALDI But was it also a mainly masculine world?

GINZBURG Yes. I had just one sister, and then there was my father who dominated an enormous space, and I had three brothers and they were . . .

SINIBALDI Energetic, as well.

GINZBURG They also dominated a big space. And I realize that I have always been dominated by someone, in general, by men. Sometimes by women too, because for a while it was my sister who dominated me; and then later, in some way, Elsa Morante. But mainly men.

FULVI It is strange that your mother would jokingly call you "my boss."

GINZBURG Yes: my mother had a much more equal relationship with my sister, and I was the true younger daughter. And she would call me "her boss." She would say too that I was dark, surly, and that I bossed her around. I think that my mother spoiled me, at least that's what my father said. And she hadn't spoiled my sister, who was in fact more important to her. Much more important because she was on the same level as her, they were very close. She wouldn't tell me what was going on in her life, but she would tell my sister.

FULVI And this made you feel isolated at times?

GINZBURG Yes, of course.

SINIBALDI Ten years after *The Things We Used to Say*, you published *Dear Michael* in '73. Ten years is a long time. Now I wouldn't like to imply that success is a burden, and that—

GINZBURG No, it isn't a burden at all.

SINIBALDI But ten years is a long time from one novel to the next.

GINZBURG Well, I had the problem of the first person—I said so earlier.

SINIBALDI And how did you get round it in the end?

GINZBURG Oh, with plays, or in *Dear Michael*, with letters.

SINIBALDI *Dear Michael* is, in fact, an epistolary novel, not completely so maybe, a halfway house, because it is an epistolary novel with a narrator.

GINZBURG Yes, the letters allow you to say "I" without actually being that "I."

SINIBALDI But is this really an idea that came to you? At a certain point you thought . . . ?

GINZBURG Well, I felt wrong using "I"; and yet I was using it— that is, I wrote a lot of articles in those years, I worked for various newspapers. And there I would use "I," because they were . . . essays.

SINIBALDI Pieces you wrote that often seem to have a casual beginning, perhaps a moment from your memory or maybe a news item, and then they expand to a dimension that is neither nonfiction nor fiction, but both at the same time.

GINZBURG They were literary articles.

SINIBALDI Yes, but very different from the traditional literary article.

GINZBURG Different, yes. But there I was making the most of saying "I!"

SINIBALDI You could say "I" freely, of course.

GINZBURG I wrote for the theater for that reason. I started to write plays during that period. Because of this business of the first person; because there, in theater, plays, you can use the first person even if you're not being yourself. This gave me a sense of freedom, because after *The Things We Used to Say*, I didn't feel like using the first person anymore, and as I don't know how to use the third person, and the second person I can't stand, so . . . [*She laughs*]. I think I wouldn't know how to write a novel with "I."

SINIBALDI In *Dear Michael* and this new epistolary technique, there's a particular presence of history, contemporary history. The events of those years take place behind the pages of *Dear Michael* in a tenuous, barely graspable way. But decisive, too—for example, they bring about the death of the young protagonist, Michael. It is a seventies book, written at the end of the sixties and the beginning of the seventies. Were you very affected by the events of those years, by the presence of history?

GINZBURG Of course, yes. Above all, I thought that young people were dying, young people were risking death. For political reasons and pseudopolitical ones; but they were in danger. And then in the prevalently female world that is the world of *Dear Michael*, there's just one straight man, who is Michael, whom we never see and who dies. Then there's the other one, who is homosexual.

SINIBALDI Oswald.

GINZBURG The father dies straightaway, Oswald is a homosexual: so it is the absence of man, yes.

SINIBALDI Did you have a maternal feeling toward the young people of those years? By maternal I meant also a degree of perplexity and suspicion about their way of life, their life choices. Reading your newspaper pieces one sometimes senses a certain diffidence as to the choices . . . these freedoms: sexual freedom, for example, or the freedom to travel. You weren't convinced by them.

GINZBURG No, no, no.

SINIBALDI There was a maternal severity about these pieces, do you agree?

GINZBURG Maybe. I wrote a . . . an essay (I don't know what to call it) called "Collective Life." And in that there's the sense of what I was feeling when faced with this changing world. It isn't that I feel the world is changing. It isn't just that the world of young people brings out a diffidence in me, it's the whole world changing. I don't think you should ever say, "The old are better than the young, or the young are better than the old." Never indulge in generational bias.

SINIBALDI "What is new is good no matter what": this seems to me one of the phrases that you would hate the most. Idolatry of the new.

GINZBURG Yes, idolatry of the new is, to me, odious.

SINIBALDI But '68 didn't excite you much either, did it?

GINZBURG "Imagination in power"—that I liked.

SINIBALDI Only that?

GINZBURG No, but it's true that I am diffident about this. It's true.

SINIBALDI *Dear Michael* is from '73 and is almost as sad as *It Happened Like This*, which came out straight after the Resistance. Now, beyond the obvious differences, it's unusual how, at times when history is suddenly injected with a new enthusiasm, you react maybe not exactly with suspicion, but certainly being aware of hidden dangers.

GINZBURG With sadness, being aware of the dangers. Well, perhaps because I am a pessimist by nature, I explain it that way. I don't know—there were things in the changing world that I didn't understand, and they put me on my guard. And then some things turned out to be justified.

SINIBALDI Some of your suspicions, you mean?

GINZBURG Some suspicions of danger turned out to be justified.

SINIBALDI Let's [conclude with] an extract from *Dear Michael*: it's one of the saddest letters, the one from Michael's mother:

August 8, 1971

Dear Philip,
Yesterday I saw you in the Spanish Square. I don't think you saw me. I was with Angelica and Flora. You were alone. Angelica thought you had aged. I don't know what I thought. You were wearing your jacket on your shoulders and made your usual gesture of rubbing your brow while you walked. You went into Babington's.

I found it extremely odd to see you pass by and not to call you, but we wouldn't really have anything in particular to say to each other. I don't much care about what is going on in your life and certainly you don't care about mine. I don't care because I am unhappy. You don't care because you are happy. Anyway, today you and I are strangers.

I know you came to the cemetery. I was not at the cemetery. Viola told me you were there. I know you told her you wanted to come and see me. Up to now you haven't come. I don't want to see you. Generally, I don't want to see anyone except my daughters with their inescapable family complications, my sister-in-law Matilde, and our friend Oswald Ventura. While I am not conscious of wanting these people's company, I miss them if I don't see them for several days. Maybe if you came to see me, I would immediately get used to you, and I don't want to accustom myself to the presence of someone who, given the circumstances, cannot be counted on. That pink little creature you married would never allow you to come often.

Because you may have become utterly stupid since we used to see each other, I hasten to explain that there is no bitterness of any kind in the words "pink little creature." Whatever jealousy or bitterness I might have felt toward you has been purged by everything that has happened to me.

Every so often I think of you. This morning I suddenly remembered the day when you and I went in your car to visit Michael, who was in camp at Courmayeur. Michael must have been about twelve at the time. I remember seeing him standing in front of his tent, nude to the waist and wearing climbing boots. I was delighted to see him looking so healthy, tanned, covered with freckles. Sometimes in town he looked so pale. He rarely went outdoors. His father never told him to go out. We drove around in the mountains and then stopped at an inn for tea. As a rule, Michael made you nervous. You didn't like him, and he didn't like you. You said he was a spoiled, willful, conceited brat. He thought that you were disagreeable. He didn't say so but clearly thought so. However, that day everything went well and peacefully without any harsh words between you. We went into a shop where they sold postcards and souvenirs. You bought him a green hat with a chamois tail. He was delighted and wore it tilted on top of his curly hair. He may have been spoiled, but he could also be amused with next to nothing. In the car he began to sing a song his father always sang. Usually that annoyed me because it reminded me of his father, about whom I felt very bitter at that time. But I was content that day, and all my bitterness grew light and sweet. The song went, "Non avemo ni canones—ni tanks ni aviones—oi Carmelà." And you knew the song and continued, "El terror de los fascistas-rumba-larumba-larumba-là." You will think it stupid, but I have written this letter to thank you for having sung with Michael that day and also for having bought him the hat with the chamois tail, which he wore for two or three years. I would like to ask you as a favor to send me the words of that song by mail if you know them. You may think it strange, but one has very minimal and odd wishes when one, in fact, desires nothing.

Adriana [9]

FOUR

THE PLAYS

MARINO SINIBALDI About halfway through the 1960s, you said, "I'm not even thinking of writing a play. I would love to, but every time I've tried to write the line 'Piero, where's my hat?' at the top of a page, I've felt deeply embarrassed and had to stop." Now, "Where's my hat?"— or rather, to be more precise, "My hat, where is it?"—is the first line in the play I Married You for the Fun of It, which you finally ended up writing. I say "ended up writing," because for autobiography, too, as we have seen, it appeared like that.

NATALIA GINZBURG Yes.

SINIBALDI You lived in total horror of autobiography and then "ended up writing" a perfect example of the form . . . The same thing happened for your plays.

GINZBURG Yes.

SINIBALDI That is, a kind of resistance to write. Then straight off, as if without thinking . . .

GINZBURG Yes, perhaps a month after making this statement, Adriana Asti came to my house and asked, "Why don't you write a play for me?" And I said no, I must have said a more or less straight no. Then I went to the countryside for a bit and wrote I Married You for the Fun of It, which began with that very line. "My hat, where is it?" It was like a bet that I was making with myself. I had no idea what story would come next, I didn't know anything. I wanted to see what came next, and which lines followed on from this one, and so I wrote this play. Which is one endless monologue, so while I was writing it I was thinking, "It's impossible to act this, because this monologue is too long." This actress is always talking, and I said it's impossible for one person to learn all these words. And then I sent it to Adriana Asti, who said that in fact she saw no problem with it, that it was fine, that she saw no problems. Then we had it read to Elsa Morante, who said it was dreadful, and then Adriana Asti got to work on it and found Gianfranco De Bosio. De Bosio from the Turin Theater Company read it and they put it on.

SINIBALDI "They put it on." Since '65 it has been put on every now and then and always, let's admit it, with considerable success.

GINZBURG Yes, it got a very harsh review straightaway from Lucio Ridenti in *Dramma*. But then they went on putting it on, and it has done well . . .

SINIBALDI You mentioned a while ago the solution to this problem of not being able to say "I" anymore. This is one of the themes, one of the "knots-in-need-of-untying" with which you experiment through the theater. In a play, you have the ability to say "I" even when talking through a male character, or through someone very different from yourself.

GINZBURG Through someone whom I thought to be different from me, yes.

SINIBALDI Let's hear a dialogue from *I Married You for the Fun of It*. The two people talking are the protagonist and Vittoria, the cleaning lady—

VITTORIA But why did you stay with him if he treated you this way?

GIULIANA Because I couldn't break away from him. I couldn't move. I was bewitched. And it's not that he treated me badly, some of the time he was good to me, it's just he was not involved, not involved . . . I had been with him more than three months and I realized I was expecting a baby.

VITTORIA Oh! What happened then?

GIULIANA I told him, and he said I was wrong, that it wasn't possible. He said it with such conviction that even I started to think it was impossible and that I had been wrong. Then one morning I woke up and he was gone. I looked everywhere for him, and he wasn't there. And I found, on the kitchen table, a letter. He said that he was going back to his parents' place for a while. He didn't leave an address. He told me not to wait for him, because he didn't know when he would be back. He told me I could feel free to stay on if I liked in the apartment, but only until September because after that he was subletting it to some Americans. I had never heard of these Americans before. He had never mentioned it to me.

VITTORIA And you? What did you do next?

GIULIANA He had left me some money in the sideboard drawer. Not much. Thirty thousand lire.

VITTORIA Nothing.

GIULIANA Yes. I started crying, and I cried for I don't know how long, I must have cried for two or three days, without eating or sleeping. Every now and then I'd go into the bathroom and wash my face with cold water. Then I'd go back to bed and start crying again. I was sure I was pregnant by then because every time I lit up a cigarette I felt really sick! I had nobody to cry with, I had to cry by myself. Elena was away on holiday, because it was summer, it was the end of July. Paoluccio, the man with the records, I tried to phone him and he didn't answer. I had nobody but the cat. Manolo hadn't taken the cat away with him. So I spent hours just stroking the cat's tail, crying, and it meowed . . . It was a very affectionate cat. It seemed to want to console me when it meowed.

VITTORIA And then?

GIULIANA Then nothing . . . at some point I stopped crying and went out to buy something to eat, for the cat and me. A few more days went by and I would walk a lot, I would walk down the streets under the hot sun because I hoped that if I walked and got tired, I might lose the baby. But the days went by and I still had the baby. And one day, I was coming in with a basket full of peaches, because I didn't feel like eating, only peaches. And I saw, in the courtyard, a girl washing a car with a sponge. The car was filthy, and the girl was filthy, too, with white shorts, covered in dirt, and a sweaty t-shirt. And the girl looked at me and I looked at her then, well, I went up to the house and after a while I heard a key turn in the lock and there before me stood the filthy girl. And I asked her, Excuse me, who are you? And the girl said, Isn't Manolo Pierfederici here? And I said, No, why? Who are you? And the girl said, I'm his wife. And I said, Topazia! And I was struck dumb.

117

VITTORIA It was Topazia!

GIULIANA Yes. If you knew how much I had thought about her, about this Topazia, how hard I'd tried to imagine what she was like! And she was like this! Some filthy girl, with fat legs, blue eyes, blond hair hanging any old way, a stripey t-shirt all covered in sweat. She said, Do you mind if I have a bath? . . . Then I said, Do you want a couple of fried eggs? And she started laughing and said, Why not? But first I'm having a bath. And she had a bath, and then she came out in Manolo's dressing gown, and she sat on the carpet in the sitting room, near to me. And then I told her everything. To another woman, to that Topazia I'd pictured in my mind, so beautiful, patronizing, proud, I wouldn't have told anything. But this one, this scruffy girl, I felt like telling everything to, just like I'm doing now with you. And I said to her, But why did you leave him? And she said, Me leave him! You must be kidding! It was he who left me. Do you see? She spoke like that. No style at all.

VITTORIA No style?

GIULIANA Not at all. And she said, He left me soon after we got married. He said he couldn't love me. I was desperate to start off with, but then I resigned myself . . . I'm a photographer. I am on the road a lot, and I take photos for a weekly magazine. Sometimes I end up here. I have a rest, have a bath, and if he's here we chat a bit, because we've stayed friends, I don't hold a grudge against him. He's a man who isn't suited to women . . .

VITTORIA And then?

GIULIANA Then we made ourselves some fried eggs, we ate all the peaches, and we went to bed. And before we went to sleep Topazia said to me, Tomorrow we'll think about it, about the baby, what you can do. If you want to keep it, I'll help you bring it up, because I've got a tipped uterus and I can't have children. And as I went to sleep I thought, "Yes, yes, I'll keep the baby! I'll work! Topazia will help me find a job! I'll become a photographer too!" But in the morning, when I woke up, I started crying and said, No, Topazia, no! I can't cope with having this baby! I've got no home, no job, no money, nothing! And she said, OK. And she took me to a Hungarian doctor, a friend of hers, and he gave me an abortion.

VITTORIA And then?

GIULIANA Then I was in bed for a few days, and Topazia looked after me. And when I was better I would go round the city with her, and I would wait for her in the car when she had her work appointments. She was a very active woman, Topazia; she did so many things. When she wasn't working she did Russian lessons, solfeggio lessons, rowing lessons, I can't tell you how many things she did. And she would go swimming at the pool. Me, when I went to the pool with her, I would get wet only up to my waist because I don't know how to swim and I'm afraid. Then I would wait for her, in the sun, on a deck chair. I had such fun with her! She made me feel great! I had never had a friend, except for Elena. The moments when I was on my own, on the deck chair, at the pool, while Topazia was swimming, I would think something and then say to myself, "I must remember what I've just thought because Topazia will be here in a moment and I'll tell it to her." And then she'd come up, Topazia, with her hair all soaked because she always swam without a cap on, and her faded blue bikini, her fat legs. Apart from her legs she had a good figure. But she had no style.

VITTORIA But what does it mean to have no style?

GIULIANA It means to have no style. To be up front, to be just as you come. I was fine with Topazia around and was having fun like I've never had with anyone else. Everything seemed easy, with her. She played things down so well. She knew how to play things down. But then Elena came back, and I told her everything, and she started crying. Elena doesn't know how to play things down . . . She kept saying, I knew it, I knew it! I knew it would end up this way! And how will you cope with a baby? and I would say, But I've had an abortion! She would say, Yes, you've had an abortion, fine, but if it happens again, how will you cope? How will you cope, the saints preserve us! And I, with Elena, I didn't have a good time. And I told her so. I would say, I don't enjoy being with you anymore! I only enjoy being with Topazia! And she was very jealous of Topazia. And she would say, You've turned nasty! now you've turned nasty as well! Then Topazia left. She had to go, for her weekly magazine, to America. So I went back to stay at Elena's . . . And that was the beginning of an awful period, because Topazia wasn't there anymore, I didn't have a job, and Elena with her long nose going on at me, telling me that perhaps I would do better to go back to Pieve di Montesecco or else I might get myself into another mess with some no-good type, and all the time I was pounding the streets just waiting for something to happen to me . . . And I was slowly falling out of love with Manolo, but falling out of love is terrible, all men seem like fools to you, you don't understand where all the lovable ones have gone. Then one day I met a friend of Topazia's, a photographer, and he took me to a party. It was a party in Via Margutta, a house with lots of tiny staircases everywhere, and with attic roofs. There were loads of people there, all sitting on these stairs, and there was pork and lentils to eat, and red wine, and people were dancing. I felt a bit lost since, apart from that photographer, I didn't know anyone. But after I'd drunk some wine, I didn't feel lost anymore, and I started to feel quite happy. And there, at that party, I met Pietro. He was sitting on the first step and was chatting to a girl with orange trousers, who I later found out was his cousin. And by the end I was completely drunk, I couldn't find the photographer anymore, and I was dancing on my own with my shoes in my hand, and my head was spinning and I fell down just next to those orange trousers. And I said, I think you should remember that you don't wear high heels with trousers! And I think you should know that getting those trousers made in that color was a really bad idea! You've go not style! And this girl was laughing, she was laughing . . . I fainted.

VITTORIA You fainted?

GIULIANA Not fainted, exactly; I just didn't know what was going on, it was the wine. And I found myself on a bed, in the hosts' bedroom . . . it was a very nice painter and his wife. And Pietro was holding my head and was making me drink coffee. I asked right off the bat if I had been sick. I would have hated to have been sick in front of such nice people. They said I hadn't. The girl with the orange trousers was fanning me with a newspaper. And then Pietro took me back home. I wasn't drunk in the slightest anymore, I was a bit embarrassed and sad. He came up with me.

VITTORIA Up to Elena's place?

GIULIANA Yes, but Elena wasn't there at the time because she'd gone to stay with a relative who'd had a stomach operation. Pietro stayed. I told him everything. Then in the morning he went to have a bath at his mother's place because our water heater was broken. And I thought, he won't come back. But he did come back, after a few hours, with a supermarket bag full of things to eat. And we lived together for ten days, until Elena came back. And in those ten days I would ask him every so often, Do you think I've got style? And he would say, No. He also thought I didn't have style. But it didn't bother me, not with him. I would tell him everything that came into my head. I never stopped talking. And every now and then he would say, Can't you keep quiet even for one minute? My head's about to burst!

VITTORIA It's true that you make a person's head fit to burst.

GIULIANA Then, when Elena was about to come back, I said to him, What a shame, now you won't be able to stay here anymore, that boring Elena's coming back . . . I mean, this is her house, after all. And he said, Yes, a shame. And I said, Marry me. Because if you don't marry me, who will?

VITTORIA And he said?

GIULIANA And he said, That's true. And he married me.

VITTORIA Well the fact is you were incredibly lucky! After what you'd been through, this was a real stroke of luck!

GIULIANA I'm not so sure.

VITTORIA It wasn't lucky? Marrying a handsome, young lawyer with all that money and you absolutely broke! You with no idea what to do to make a living?

GIULIANA Yes, I had no idea. I had all these debts. No job. Plus I don't have any great desire to hold a job. I said to him, to Pietro, Yes, I'll marry you, but I'm afraid I don't love you! With you it isn't like it was with Manolo! With Manolo it was as if I had been bewitched. And he said, It's not a problem. And when Elena came back, I said to her, Guess what, I've found someone who'll marry me. And she said, Someone who'll marry you? Oh, not another mess you're getting yourself into! Oh, poor me! The saints preserve us! She couldn't believe it, that there was someone who was going to marry me. And when Pietro turned up, she stared at him with those little eyes of hers, pointing her little nose like she wanted to sting him. Then she said, Well, who knows, maybe this one isn't a saints preserve us. This one seems like a man with his head screwed on! And I said, But I'm not bewitched by him! And she said, Go to hell!

VITTORIA She had a point.

GIULIANA Maybe.

VITTORIA Oh God, it's late, I must get on with the cooking. He'll be back soon and lunch isn't ready.

GIULIANA You can tell him it was my fault, that I got you talking.

VITTORIA Got me talking? I hardly opened my mouth! You did all the talking. You really can talk away! Do you always talk like that?

GIULIANA Always.

VITTORIA Doesn't talking that much make you thirsty?

GIULIANA Yes. Bring me a glass of milk.

VITTORIA You want milk now? It's midday!

GIULIANA I love milk.

SINIBALDI How many plays have you written?

GINZBURG Ten.

SINIBALDI I would like to ask Masolino D'Amico, theater critic and historian, who is here with us now to help us to identify, within the context of the times in which they were written— from the sixties until today, important times for the history of theater—the importance of Natalia Ginzburg's theatrical works.

MASOLINO D'AMICO At the first Spoleto Festival, Giancarlo Menotti invited Italian writers to do a few pages, some short pieces, for the festival album. Many sent things in, and some were quite good but nothing came of it. When this play arrived by Natalia Ginzburg, it seemed that it wasn't even a play. Because it was almost a monologue and because there was hardly any action, it was going against the tide as far as the theater of the time was concerned. Theater then was heading toward an emphasis on gesture and image, not on the word. It needed a special actress to insist she wanted to do it because I'm not sure how many actors of the time would have been keen to talk so much. And yet, mysteriously, the thing worked. Immediately, then, you had this faction of theater people who were happy to have texts, because of course directors love to be successful, actors love to be successful, and if there's a thing that works, the theater people will do it. So it imposed itself in spite of everything, it imposed itself by its own efforts, because the public loved it and because actors loved doing it. Strangely enough—and this was something else that people talked a lot about at the time—it was immediately in demand abroad. It's a play that traveled well, something that no other contemporary Italian author except for Eduardo had achieved. It was put on with much pomp and glory at the National Theater by Laurence Olivier. It did well there; people liked it, and they made a film version. *The Advertisement* was then done by Visconti in Italy, the following year . . .

SINIBALDI You mentioned how a more gesture-based theater was dominant at the time. There were also traditions of which Natalia Ginzburg was in some way unaware when she recovered an idea of theater as words, communication. After that, it seems that her characters are not unaware of the problems of contemporary theater. For example, they talk a lot, but they communicate very little. That is, they too are close to incommunicability; they are alienated characters in some way, with history, without epos; they are just that, noncommunicative. They are just frenetic, they seem euphoric but not vital.

D'AMICO Natalia Ginzburg did a very simple thing. She did not write a play, she didn't give a structure to this play. We could say it is traditional theater in the sense that these people talk rather than act, but traditional theater has its rules. It is structured—there are acts and the ends of acts, there are various scenes, there are climaxes, there are lots of characters. But in her plays, all this is completely ignored. What Natalia has done is do the thing she knows: she tells us about a character, she puts a character there and makes him talk. The big novelty is that there is a character. We go there to see a person, to see a person move, to recognize a person. For a long time these plays went on having just one person and talking about characters who aren't there. There's always this presence, which there is also in her narrative, of the important absentee. In her last play, which in my opinion is her best, we get to have two characters. So, at the end of a lengthy evolution, we've managed to double them—plus another who isn't there but who is discussed all the time. So progress is made a little at a time.

SINIBALDI Just to clarify, this last play is *The Advertisement*.

D'AMICO But the big novelty is that people rediscovered the pleasure they had found in going to see the classics, in seeing pieces of life, hearing people, recognizing something and not seeing abstractions. Which all goes down very well in the theater.

SINIBALDI There's room for everything.

D'AMICO There's room for the gesture, there's room for a small province of the theater, a select society. At the beginning it seemed very local, very small, almost uniquely Roman or, rather, Roman by immigration. But then it turned out that it worked in translation, it held its own. So, as the old saying goes, if someone does something that stands up in a small context, then it can multiply into infinity, it can go on being valid.

SINIBALDI So, Natalia said that there's room for everything in theater.

GINZBURG There's room for everything.

SINIBALDI In your theoretical text, which is called "Il teatro è parola" (Theater is word), you speak passionately in favor of the theater of the word. Then you describe the anger you felt when you saw Eugenio Barba's *Odin*, which was theater as removed as possible from the word and as close as possible to the gesture. So what are your tastes in theater?

GINZBURG I think that there's room for everything. I think that the avant-garde was wrong when it said that one thing kills another.

SINIBALDI Does that go for theater as well as for literature and for politics, for example? In whatever context, does the avant-garde make this mistake?

GINZBURG Well, of course, also in politics. But in theater it's plainer to see, and in narrative, in art, it's plain to see. Why must one thing kill another? There's room enough for all of them, for the new things and for how things used to be. And I go on to say there that I was going to the theater to see Goldoni's plays, for example.

D'AMICO Particularly in this current period, because this is the era that has given everything back its true value. There has never been a period like the modern one, in which we can appreciate gothic, Romanesque, romantic, decadent, classical . . . We appreciate every-thing, we give everything its due, our valuers let everything through. There may be a fashion at any one time, but we have the means of understanding all forms of language.

SINIBALDI If anything, the only new language is the one that spreads, recovers, mixes . . .

D'AMICO Of course, at its root. It's true that this pleasure in sitting and listening to a man or woman speak is threatened by the fact that ours is an era that has discovered the impact of the visual, which is much more efficient at rapidly transmitting a message. And so all the advertising, the TV, and so on. But in the face of this continuous aggression, the will to listen is still very powerful. Anyone who slips into this space has no regrets. Now in Natalia we have the example of a writer who has transferred her language into sound, and she found some actors who knew how to do it. She has been lucky always to have really good actors.

GINZBURG Very lucky.

D'AMICO She has written for actresses and these actresses have re-warded her well. That extract we heard with Adriana Asti was mar-velous; she's an extraordinary actress.

SINIBALDI Let's listen to another extract from I Married You for the Fun of It. This time the dialogue is between Pietro and Giuliana, that is, Renzo Montagnani and Adriana Asti.

PIETRO [Picking something up from the floor] What's this? My pajamas? How come Vittoria hasn't done the room yet?

GIULIANA How could she do the room, can't you see I'm in bed?

PIETRO And don't you think you should get up?

GIULIANA I had a chat with Vittoria. I told her about my life. She listened really closely, didn't miss a word. Whereas you, when I talk, you don't listen. This morning you went out while I was talking. Even though I was saying something important.

PIETRO Really? What were you saying to me?

GIULIANA I was saying that I can't see, between us two, a real reason for living together.

PIETRO You were saying that to me?

GIULIANA Yes.

PIETRO We've got no real reason for living together? You think that?

GIULIANA I do. I find you a very frivolous person. Marrying me, you showed how frivolous you are.

PIETRO I'm not at all frivolous. I'm someone who always knows what he's doing . . .

GIULIANA Whereas I never know what I'm doing. I go from one blunder to the next. But how can you say that, that you always know what you're doing? So far you haven't done anything. Or nothing important, anyway. Getting married was the first important thing in your life.

PIETRO Before I met you I had been on the verge of marrying at least another eighteen times. I always backed out. Because I found in those women something that made me shiver. I found, deep in their spirit, a sting. They were wasps. When I met you, who aren't a wasp, I married you.

GIULIANA There's something offensive, I find, in the way you say I'm not a wasp. You mean I'm some little house-trained animal, harmless, sweet? A butterfly?

PIETRO I said you weren't a wasp. I didn't say you were a butterfly. You're always so quick to describe yourself in such gracious terms.

GIULIANA I don't find butterflies gracious. I find them horrible. I

125

almost prefer wasps. I'm offended that you think I've got no sting. It's true, but it offends me.

PIETRO . . . Right now I advise you to get up, wash up, and come and eat. The soup will be well and truly cooked by now.

GIULIANA There is no soup. And I don't know if I'm going to bother washing. When I'm feeling sad I don't feel like washing. You've made me feel sad.

PIETRO I've made you sad? Me?

GIULIANA You came back from that funeral all full of yourself . . . You're full of yourself, so self-confident, you're patronizing, and very unpleasant. You talk about me as if you know me inside out.

PIETRO Well, I do know you inside out.

GIULIANA . . . How can you say that when we don't even know why we got married! We spend our whole time wondering why we did it!

PIETRO You do. I don't. I don't wonder about anything. You're a person with mixed-up ideas. I'm not. I see things clearly. I see things clearly and far ahead.

GIULIANA See what a high opinion you have of yourself! Such self-confidence! "I see clearly and far ahead!" I'm telling you we're in a thick fog! We're completely surrounded by fog! We can't even see to the end of our nose!

PIETRO Shall I turn on the bath for you?

GIULIANA What?

PIETRO Shall I turn on the bath for you? if you have a bath, perhaps your head will clear. Having a bath is good. It detoxifies. It clears your head.

GIULIANA You're not some kind of hygiene freak, are you? Tell me now because I can't stand hygiene freaks.

PIETRO Of course. I'm a hygiene freak. Didn't you know?

GIULIANA I don't think I'll bother washing. I'm too down . . . [She goes into the bathroom. The sound of water running into the bathtub. As she reenters] I find that marriage is an infernal institution! To have to live together, always, for all one's life! Why did I marry you? What have I done? What was I thinking, when I took you on?

PIETRO You've decided to have a bath?

GIULIANA Didn't you tell me I had to?

PIETRO It wasn't an order. It was a suggestion.

GIULIANA Sure! As if you'd ever order me around! . . . "I know you inside out!" "I see clearly and far ahead!" And what if you didn't know me at all? if you'd made a mistake? if suddenly you found out I'm full of hidden poison? Then what? What would you do then?

PIETRO I'd leave you. It's logical.

GIULIANA Logical! [*She goes into the bathroom then comes back*] The hell it's logical. Now you've married me and you keep me, you keep me just as I am! Even if I'm nothing like you thought I was, you have to keep me all the same, for always! Didn't I just say that marriage is a diabolical institution?

PIETRO Careful. You're treading on my pajamas.

GIULIANA I'm treading on them because I want to tread on them! Because I can't stand you!

SINIBALDI I want to ask Masolino D'Amico to help us look more closely at the humor here, which has a vaguely alienating quality yet enriches the tonalities of the text. In general, does the particular type of irony that Natalia Ginzburg uses in her texts serve to make them more appealing to the public?

D'AMICO Well, I wouldn't talk about this irony like another added ingredient. These texts aren't conceivable without this ironic dimension—but I wouldn't quite call it ironic. Humor is a part of these texts, or rather, the keynote of these texts is that the characters, in a funny, happy, playful way try to laugh at their misfortunes.

SINIBALDI They manage to laugh at their misfortunes.

D'AMICO Yes, they make their misfortunes funny, or rather, they don't manage to laugh themselves but they manage to make others laugh. It's the only way they can tell these stories, because if they told them straight they would be terrible.

SINIBALDI So pathetic as to be terrible.

D'AMICO They could be pathetic and perhaps even are pathetic. But when—and occasionally it has happened—they are staged without highlighting the ironic component, they are a disaster. They don't work even for a second. Laughter is a must. I think we've had proof of that in the pieces we've just heard.

SINIBALDI Yes. Natalia, were you happy when you wrote them?

GINZBURG No, no. I wasn't at all happy when I wrote them. This is the happiest of my plays; the others are darker. *The Advertisement* is the darkest play, though, with comic twists to it as well.

SINIBALDI *The Advertisement* is the next play, written about a year later.

GINZBURG Adriana did this one too, in Italy.

SINIBALDI Let's listen to it. But first I wanted to ask you about the particular use of language. Was this some of the difficulty for you in writing for theater?

GINZBURG No.

SINIBALDI What I mean is, is there a distance between spoken and written language? Obviously, the writer who is involved in plays has to move . . .

GINZBURG Well, I found that it gave me no problems. I just got on with it; I saw at once that the language was not a problem for me. What *was* a problem was the progression within the play, making things happen . . . seeing how things came about, without any help. It's easy to tell a story in a novel. Telling a story in a play is hard.

SINIBALDI In the preface to I Married You for the Fun of It, Natalia Ginzburg wrote, "Nothing happens in this text, and it doesn't have any meaning." D'Amico, was it normal, in your opinion, to say such things in the mid-sixties?

D'AMICO The same has been said of many of the more famous plays in the history of the theater. It was said of Oscar Wilde's The Importance of Being Earnest. The critics wrote, "The only thing they talk about is cucumber sandwiches, and nothing happens!" The truth is that what happens in the theater is theater. You've sat there for an hour and a half or two hours, and this has all taken its own shape, and that is what you go to see. And it isn't true that nothing happens. At the end, the characters have understood things about themselves, relationships have changed. And above all, they have told us, we have been present. They are three-dimensional characters, and we end up knowing these people we didn't know at all before.

SINIBALDI Perhaps it is that very few changes take place in the psychology of the characters.

D'AMICO Yes, no such events happen there, on the stage, in front of us. But this is true also of classical theater. In Sophocles' plays, too, nothing happens.

SINIBALDI Or it has already happened.

D'AMICO Nothing happens—they tell you about it.

GINZBURG Which "doesn't have any meaning," because it has no message to offer.

SINIBALDI That was the sense in which you said, "It doesn't have any meaning."

D'AMICO For me it isn't true that there's no message there. You see a person who is facing life, you have an example of irreducible vitality, you see (in the case of I Married You for the Fun of It or of The Advertisement) these women who stay afloat, who are knocked about, who get back up again, who take the blows, who manage to . . . I don't know, maintain a vitality. Not that it is a lesson that you can follow, but . . .

GINZBURG Yes, the message, if you like, is this. But perhaps it isn't a real message; I mean, it is something that I didn't know when I wrote it.

SINIBALDI Let's listen now to an extract from The Advertisement, which is the second of your plays and which also enjoyed the success we spoke of earlier. There is this new, darker tone about it, that's for sure, and yet there's also—to confirm Masolino D'Amico's viewpoint—something going on, a transformation taking place. There's a meeting between the two women that changes them both, especially the young one in whom we see this vitality just mentioned. Something happens, relationships cross over, become more complicated, are changed. We will hear the last part of the play The Advertisement.

TERESA . . . How a man can ruin you! He ruins you then he leaves you there.

ELENA Forgive him . . .

TERESA I could have married someone else if I hadn't met him that day. I was so young and pretty. There were so many men after me. I could have picked a simple, quiet, nice man, had an ordered and regular existence. Instead . . . What a disaster! He ruined me. He destroyed me. Then he left, just like someone who tramples across a lawn then goes. "You are nothing," he said to me. "You are not, for me, a person. You have betrayed me, but I don't care at all . . ." What will I do? Tell me, what will I do now? What else is there left for me to do but shoot myself through the heart? I've got one, you know . . . a pistol. I've had it ever since we had the villa in Rocca di Papa. Because I thought I was afraid to sleep there alone at night, when he was away . . .

ELENA And where is this pistol now?

TERESA What does it matter where it is? I've got it. I've got it in my bag. One day I'll shoot myself. Then you won't even need an annulment . . .

ELENA Give it to me, the gun.

TERESA No way.

ELENA Give me your bag.

TERESA No way.

ELENA Throw it away, the gun! I'm begging you, Teresa, I'm begging you, throw it away!

TERESA Yes, I'll throw it away.

ELENA I have to get dressed. It's late. I have to shut the suitcase. He'll be here soon. You won't be alone, Teresa! I'll come and see you all the time, he'll come and see you all the time! We two will always love you very much! [*She hugs her*]

TERESA Yes.

ELENA I have to go and get dressed. [*She goes out*]

[*Teresa goes into her room. Then into Elena's room. The stage is empty. A shot is heard.*]

TERESA [*She runs to the phone and dials a number*] Hello, Lorenzo! Lorenzo! Come quickly, for God's sake, come quickly, I've killed her! I didn't mean to, I didn't mean to, but I killed her, she died, she died instantly! For God's sake, Lorenzo, get over here, get over here!

[*She bursts into tears. A doorbell rings. Teresa dries her eyes with her hands. She opens the door. Giovanna comes in.*]

GIOVANNA Hello. I phoned a few hours ago. I've come about the advertisement in the paper. My name's Giovanna Ricciardi.

ELENA Which advertisement? I put three in.

GIOVANNA The room.[1]

D'AMICO I saw, reading Natalia's introduction to *The Advertisement*, that you say you wrote eleven plays.

GINZBURG It's ten, I made a mistake.

D'AMICO Where are these ten plays? I only know four or five, I think.

GINZBURG There are two volumes; Einaudi is about to publish one.

D'AMICO Right, they haven't all been performed.

GINZBURG Some have been performed abroad, on foreign radio, but they're not all performed.

SINIBALDI Why is that, in your opinion?

D'AMICO Well, it's hard to say; I'd have to read them first. But it's very odd, what happens to plays in Italy. It's very hard for an Italian author to get his work put on. Flaiano had enormous difficulties even though now (after his death) they put his plays on. But in general it's really not easy. So Natalia has been very—

GINZBURG —lucky.

D'AMICO Lucky, in one way. Starting with the actor, who is very important, or rather, a motivated actor who commissions a text from you for him to put on. Adriana Asti is a minor star, she was able to take it to the stage, and this is a very sound beginning. To write plays in the abstract, without someone backing you, is very risky. Few people do it, and those few end up competing with each other. They submit their work for these awards, they win some small prize. But it's very unlikely that the plays will ever get staged.

GINZBURG Then I was very lucky with Giulia Lazzarini who put on *The Advertisement* for Strehler at the Piccolo Teatro.

D'AMICO Well, at this point in your career these discussions no longer apply, but of course, again with Lazzarini you were stimulated, forced even into writing this other text, which I maintain is the best you've ever written—a piece of sublime craftsmanship, a perfect show, wonderfully done, not only Lazzarini.

GINZBURG No, no, Haber is excellent, too.

D'AMICO Yes, the actor as well, Alessandro Haber. As we were saying, it is a text between characters who are on the same level, a dialogue between two people who instead of telling their tale one at a time, both tell their tale at the same time. Three acts, with a progression. It's also a text that plays a lot with the public, because it's a text written in an extraordinary way, in the way it's constructed, because these three acts carry this story on in a very subtle way. They drop, then pick up again certain small allusions that slowly develop. So it is made with great cunning from one point of view, but then there is also this candid approach that I can't help but admire. For example, there are no ends of acts. Natalia says, "I can't write ends of acts," and so it just goes out.

SINIBALDI Every act.

D'AMICO . . . which in fact shows great refinement, because it is a play that doesn't need it. You sit and listen as if it were written with the greatest cunning.

SINIBALDI *The Advertisement* is dedicated to a young director who put on . . .

GINZBURG Luca Coppola, yes. Luca Coppola put on *Dialogo* (Dialogue). He did it very well. He was a good friend of mine, we were very close, and he did this in a way I really liked. Then he died, he and an actor, Giancarlo Prati, were killed in Mazara del Vallo, that was his awful end. A death similar to Pasolini's. And the two actors went on performing *Dialogo*, they still put it on in Milan. It did well.

SINIBALDI *The Advertisement* is the last piece you wrote for the theater, so that means your tenth play (just to be sure of the statistics!). But let's hear an extract from La parrucca (The wig), in which some of these motifs, especially the centrality of a female character, are absolute. It is a monologue by a woman in a bare and anonymous hotel room. And the mode of communication is also anonymous, one long phone call, a desolate human voice, but also frenetic, euphoric, betrayed by the customary figure of a man who is trying to run away. Verbosity, solitude: some of the motifs running through Natalia Ginzburg's theater seem to be summed up in this monologue:

[*A woman is sitting on the bed. She picks up the receiver.*]

Hello? Miss? I'd like to be put through to Milan 80 18 96. And I'd asked for an egg to drink. I was brought the tea but not the egg. The tea was like water. Yes. It doesn't matter. No, my husband doesn't take tea, he'll have milky coffee but later on. So could you get me the Milan number? Sorry? The number I just gave you. Oh God, I can't find it now. 80 18 96. No, I don't want to dial direct. I told you before I don't want to dial direct.

[*She stands in front of a mirror and starts to put on make-up. In the next room, someone whistles.*]

Massimo? Well, I've asked for Milan. Stop whistling. My skin's so dry, yellow . . . how horrible. No wonder—I slept so badly. The mattress was so lumpy. And I was cold. The blankets in this hotel are so thin. And by the way, my nose hurts. It's swollen. And keeps bleeding. Massimo, there's still blood on the cotton wool. I can't cope with the sight of my own blood. Other people's is OK. If you dare hit me again I'm leaving and I won't come back. My jaw hurts, so does my nose. For God's sake, get out of that bloody bath. You always look dirtier than when you got in, anyway. Strange. Whereas me, I look clean even if I haven't had a bath. This wig has had it. It looks like an old rag. The way you sent it flying. It's still got mud on it. What a shame. It was a present from you. The only present you ever gave me in six years of marriage. Because you're mean. You're mean with me. But very generous toward yourself. You bought yourself that jacket. Given our finances, it was hardly the thing to do. And it doesn't suit you. You're too short to be wearing raspberry pink velvet. Bloody hotel! I ordered an egg to drink and they're not bringing it.

[*The phone rings*]

That'll be my mother.

Hello, Mom? Hi, Mom. I've been asking to be put through for an hour. I don't dial direct because Massimo doesn't want me to. He's mean. But he isn't mean when it comes to his clothes; I was just saying that he's bought himself a raspberry-pink velvet jacket, really awful. Him being so small, I can't tell you what it looks like. You haven't seen him for ages—he's grown his hair. You've never seen him with long hair. He's got those two enormous tufts of golden moustache, then more golden hair down to his shoulders. Yes, I haven't phoned you for ages, but I did write. Didn't I write and tell you he'd grown his hair? How odd.

Do you know where I'm calling from? From Montesauro. A village on top of a hill. It's snowing. We're in a hotel called Collodoro. No, it isn't a good hotel. Quite the opposite. I'd asked for an egg and it still hasn't come. I had to put my jumper on over my night shirt because it's freezing here. What are we doing here? I don't even know myself. No girls. The girls are in Rome. They're with the woman who looks after the house. No, but they're very happy with her. She's a cheerful woman. Always singing. Yes, I can trust her. She's good. She can't do anything but she's good. Me, lucky? Lucky why? With her? Yes, I'm lucky with her but very unlucky with everything else.

Exactly. A good idea that we didn't bring the girls as well. Because it's snowing. So we left so as to go to Todi, but then on the motorway the Renault stopped, it made an awful noise and then it stopped. It was snowing, we were in real trouble. So we picked up our cases and the pictures and started walking. We must have walked for half an hour. Then eventually we found a service station. My feet were soaked through. No boots. Why not, because I didn't bring them, in Rome when we set off it was lovely weather. I had my buckskin jacket and my long black skirt. No tights. From there we phoned a mechanic and they towed the Renault away. It looks as though it needs a new battery. The mechanic recommended this hotel. Last night we had some chewy meatballs for dinner then went straight to bed. My feet were like ice cubes. Massimo was furious as hell. He took his bed into the bathroom. He says he sleeps better when he's alone.

Mom. I rang you for something specific. We need money. We came away from Rome with hardly any. Why, because we didn't know that the battery would break. If you wire me some money,

200,000 lire . . . well, yes. I'm sorry. I'll try and pay you back. Eighty thousand alone is for the battery and the rest we could do with. More than could do with . . . we can't do without. When we left it was Saturday, we couldn't get to the bank. Not that we've got much in the bank. Almost nothing. We were planning on getting to Todi that same evening and we'd have found a place to stay there, we've got friends in Todi.

FIVE

INTERLOCUTORS

MARINO SINIBALDI Today I would like to talk to Natalia Ginzburg and to a guest, Clorinda Gallo (everyone calls her Dinda, so we'll do the same), about Natalia Ginzburg's relationships with her friends, interlocutors, the critics whose opinion she values, the people she consults. Do you often get others to read what you write? I don't know if it signifies great generosity or great insecurity.

NATALIA GINZBURG Great insecurity.

SINIBALDI But then, you don't always take into account what people say, even when it's negative.

GINZBURG No. Not always.

SINIBALDI In a text that is, by the way, called "Interlocutors," you talk about four people whose opinion you regularly seek. Let's hear it:

I have, perhaps, four interlocutors at the moment; my friend C.; two female friends of mine, L. and A.; my eldest son. Among the people I see fairly often there are perhaps others, too, whom I'd like to use as interlocutors. But since sometimes I've worried that it would bother them or I had the sensation that they were not that keen to read what I had written, I therefore dropped the idea of them as interlocutors. Because interlocutors must never say no.

Besides, it's vital that interlocutors should never judge us to be useless, as writers. Given that our fear of being useless or, rather, of writing useless things, often hides within us with a subtle and painful insistence, we must have interlocutors who protect us from this fear.

As for my eldest son, I thought for a long time that I couldn't use him as an interlocutor because children can't be interlocutors, given that they tend to be hypercritical of us and punishingly severe. If this isn't the case then the opposite happens, and that's worse—that is, consciously or subconsciously, they tend to put us on a pedestal. Whereas at a certain time I realized that this son of mine, in his own strange way, is an interlocutor for me. This is how: I offer him what I've written, he reads it and immediately responds with a stream of insults and abusive remarks. The strange thing is that his abusive remarks don't upset me at all and make me want to laugh. He wants to laugh as well, but this doesn't stop him from reeling off his insults with a savage and amused bullishness. Laughter and happiness pour out of his coal-black eyes, from his wild, black, hairy head. I think that insulting me is one of the pleasures of his life. Listening to his insults is certainly one of the pleasures of mine.

Just what advantages I get from such a flow of insults is hard to say. It isn't criticism, it's insults. Basically he finds me a sickly and sentimental writer. But that is a rather softened and watered-down version of how he rants about my writing. How on earth I should feel revived and remotivated and pushed on to write more after so many insults is a mystery to me. I have the secret idea that sometimes what I write in some way makes him curious, intrigues him, and doesn't wholly displease him. He doesn't feel contempt for me. In his insults, contempt is totally absent.

My friend C. is a critic. He is in every way the perfect interlocutor. In fact, he is not only an interlocutor to me but to a range of other people who write. He is, as a human being, restless, not at all patient. With people who write, however, he is blessed with an extreme patience. Besides which, he has the strange gift of motivating and stimulating, in his fellow man, ideas and the desire to write.

I would go even so far as to say that you only have to see him come into a room to get ideas to write. You always have the feeling that, once out the door, he will forget you straightaway, so as to dedicate his attention to other people and writings that he'll come across. But that doesn't matter. In some way he stays faithful to friends, because, after long absences, he picks up the dialogue again as if it had never been interrupted.

Neither my friend C. nor my son can be given my plays to read. My son generally gives such negative comments that, if I listened to him, I would tear up all my plays into tiny pieces. For my plays, he doesn't use up his streams of insults. He says it all in a few words. He laughs and shakes his black, shaggy head. He says, generally, that they are plays that make you "sleep standing up." Besides which he says that he doesn't like the theater and that, when he goes to the theater, he is so bored it almost makes him itch and sweat. On occasion he has gone, at my request and out of pure kindness, to see plays of mine that were being put on, and he has told me that he was sweating the whole way through. As for my friend C., I have given him my plays to read every now and then; he has taken them home and then promptly lost them. I have never been sure whether he lost them before reading them or after. Either way, he has never made any real comment on them, and it is clear that either they didn't interest him or they didn't appeal to him.

My only interlocutor for my plays is my friend A. She has always given really useful opinions. From what she says I know that she has given it serious attention. Attention is a precious gift, and it isn't true that you can find it on any street corner. I think that anyone who writes is never wrong as far as another man's attention is concerned, that is, he knows straightaway when someone has not managed to give the piece his full attention and has instead skimmed through it in a flabby and distracted way. Based on the attention our interlocutors pay we can up to a point estimate whether what we have written will be worthy of, will receive a bit of attention or nothing. The fact that my friend A. doesn't have, in terms of plays, a particular competence and perhaps has a limited knowledge of theater is of no importance to me. She maybe can't give me a final judgment on my plays, but she can say that one seems the best or the worst. I think it should be up to me to make a final judgment on my plays, even if it is perhaps rough-and-ready, and only so far as one human being can reach a judgment about himself. Such a final judgment I have never reached about my plays, and this seems a bad sign to me. It seems like a sign of immaturity. When someone has reached a minimum of maturity in his writing, he should know what he has written and why. Interlocutors can't help him with this. Interlocutors are useful in the moments of something being written and immediately after, just as when a person climbs to the top of a mountain, he needs a sip of water or a hand behind his back or just the sensation that somewhere near him there is a living breath or footstep. You don't really ask interlocutors for a critical, lucid, and disenchanted judgment so much as for a kind of participation, a support in words and thoughts to our solitary writing.

Some days ago, coming back to Rome from the country, I had just finished writing one piece and I wanted to start another. I had no interlocutors and felt the lack of this. There was A., but what I had written wasn't a play, and A. is good mostly for plays. There was my friend L., but she was leaving for Cappadocia. She was very caught up in preparations for departure, flying through the city with her aquiline profile. I managed to sit her down on the sofa at my house for half an hour and give her what I'd written to read. She said a few quick words, which were rather precious to me. This friend of mine is not very useful for my fiction or for my plays; she is precious for reflective pieces because she is so quick to see true from false. When she had gone, I was left alone with my second son. He isn't usually, as far as my writing goes, an interlocutor of mine because I always have the feeling that he despises me as a writer, that is, that he finds me basically useless. I always have the impression with him that anything in the world that isn't mathematics, economics, politics seems to him, fundamentally, futile and useless. The fact that he isn't, as far as my writing is concerned, one of my interlocutors does not in any way limit our relationship: I can talk to him about every other kind of thing. That evening I asked him all the same to read what I had written, and I gave him my pages. He read it, laughed a bit, and said that it was "not bad." These words made me feel quite euphoric. The next day, I quickly jotted down another piece. It was on the privileges of class. I had lots of doubts and a few strong hopes. When he came back that evening, I gave him my new pages to read. He has never, unlike my other son, covered me in abusive remarks; he tends to be more reserved and cautious when commenting on my writing, and also very careful not to cause me pain. In fact, he doesn't cause me pain; and yet almost always, after he has commented on something, I feel as useless and futile as a flowery silk neck scarf.

He has just started growing a beard and while he read he stroked his beard, and from the way he stroked his beard I could see that he didn't like what I had written at all. His comments were gentle, cheerfully delivered and inexorable. He told me that I had confused capitalism with industrial society. I didn't realize I had spoken either about capitalism or about industrial society. I was dumbstruck.

I had bought him some pajamas and some shirts. He said that he would never wear those shirts because they were "textured," that is, they had in the weave of the fabric the thinnest lines running through, almost invisible. I hadn't seen this, having bought them in the evening. And he didn't like the pajamas either because one pair was green, and the other was pink. He only likes blue.

The next day I was cross with him, partly because he had annihilated without remission my writing and partly because he had gone out and left on the sofa the shirts and pajamas that he had told me he would take back and exchange. I thought that, seeing as he generally dresses in a rather shabby way, nobody would have ever guessed that he had something against "textured" shirts and that he could distinguish one fabric from another. I thought that his antipathy toward "textured" shirts must probably come from the fact that he thought them "frivolous." I thought that he had the wrong idea about frivolousness and seriousness, not only as far as fabric and clothes were concerned but in general. All the same, looking at one of the pairs of pajamas that I had bought him, the pink one, I saw that it was in fact a wine-colored pink, rather revolting. I read what I had written again and found it repulsive. It emitted a sickly smell.

I loathed myself so totally and so deeply that I felt I would never be able to write again. I had broken my ties with the world and found myself on a street littered with so many obstacles that I didn't know how to walk.

When my son came home, I told him he was right. I showed him the piece of writing folded in four and tied up with a rubber band. I had decided to drop it, push it to the back of a drawer. He had come back early to go out again and exchange the pink pajamas. He hadn't forgotten those pajamas. He went out and came back a bit later with a blue pair.

I was grateful to him for not having allowed me to attribute any importance to that piece of mine and for having ordered me, with rather a gentle approach, to drop it. Now, slowly and with difficulty, I had to move the piles of dead thoughts out of my road.

SINIBALDI Dinda Gallo collaborated with you on an anthology for secondary schools, La vita (Life), an anthology that Garboli claims is a basic tool for understanding Natalia Ginzburg. A strange anthology, I would say, because it is at once scholastic and lively. It's personal, original, with a straightforward approach and no suffocating apparatus of precooked culture that now seems an intrinsic part of books for schools. Perhaps for this reason, it has had difficulty in being adopted.

GINZBURG It didn't do at all well, but it was fun. We got enormous pleasure out of making it. I did the introductions, Dinda wrote the notes, and together we chose which pieces to include. We would choose long extracts, sometimes long extracts from novels, and lots of poetry. There was just one point of disagreement between us. She said I put in things that were too tragic, too dark.

DINDA GALLO I've been a teacher, so I have an idea of what school-children like, and it seemed to me that some of the things were a bit demanding, and painful especially. But the anthology was good in the end, very good. And we really did have a great time making it, because it gave us a chance to reread so many things that we both liked and to compare our tastes. We think the anthology is wonderful. The fact that others aren't so keen on it is neither here nor there.

GINZBURG Pampaloni liked it, too; he was the one who asked us to compile it. But it didn't do well.

SINIBALDI Seeing as we want to promote it to the end, it's published by De Agostini.

GINZBURG Then the people at De Agostini wanted to revive it. The anthology is divided by subject headings like "love," "birth," "death," "pain," "laughter," "food," "water." Then they wrote to us saying they wanted to keep the notes, the introductions, and some of the choices, but they wanted to change these headings. Where there was "war" they wanted to put "epic"; or where there was "love" they wanted to put "feelings"; where there was "fables" they wanted to put "fable."

SINIBALDI You mean they wanted to substitute the abstract for the concrete.

GINZBURG So we said that we didn't agree.

SINIBALDI Dinda, what does the idea of an interlocutor mean to you? Niccolò, your husband, was one.

GALLO It isn't so easy to say. But I do believe that to be true interlocutors you need a very close relationship with someone: to know that person very well.

SINIBALDI But in your opinion, is it really insecurity that makes Natalia Ginzburg seek all these opinions?

GALLO I don't think so.

GINZBURG Well, yes, a bit out of insecurity: I want to have support, someone behind me. But even Cesare Garboli uses Dinda as an interlocutor.

SINIBALDI So it is a circular chain.

GINZBURG —because he gets her to read his work.

GALLO Yes, yes.

GINZBURG Always! He sends things, proofs to her, so it isn't only me.

GALLO Well, I don't judge. I'm just an interlocutor out of friendship. They like to get me to read their work before it comes out.

SINIBALDI You mean you don't judge its worth?

GALLO I don't think they take too much notice of what I say.

GINZBURG That's not true! It may not be harsh criticism, but it's support.

SINIBALDI But I have the impression that a writer is essentially alone, that he can't much rely on others.

GINZBURG That's true. But I had Gabriele [Ginzburg's second husband—*trans.*] as interlocutor for many years; I would always get him to read every little piece I wrote. My children said he was too kind because he wasn't severe, whereas they were very severe. He stimulated me to keep going.

SINIBALDI What do you think, Dinda? Doesn't it imply an extraordinary compliance, welcoming criticism in this way, the dismissive reviews, Elsa Morante's vehement attacks, even the ferocity of one's offspring?

GALLO I would say there's a great strength in her, not insecurity. As a result, if Carlo, her eldest son, tells her that her plays make him fall asleep it may not please her, but it doesn't affect her greatly.

GINZBURG No.

SINIBALDI How can it not affect her when someone falls asleep in front of her plays?

GALLO It isn't the case. Actually, people enjoy themselves and laugh!

GINZBURG Carlos's comment on my last play was, "Not bad." The way he says something is good is by saying it's "not bad." It's the best thing I've heard him say about anything of mine, "Not bad."

GALLO But Cesare, too, has been known to tear your work to pieces, hasn't he?

GINZBURG Cesare, YES! Yes, yes, a lot. Cesare . . . well, yes, he didn't mind the last play either.

GALLO No, he liked it a lot. But, I must say, his criticisms are generally constructive.

GINZBURG I do listen to him. When I wrote *The Manzoni Family*, he made a lot of suggestions.

GALLO Well, he got cross.

GINZBURG He did get cross: I remember one evening he found that I had made a mistake, I can't remember exactly. I wrote a lot of *The Manzoni Family* with Dinda. She was the one who suggested I write it. I was vaguely interested in this family, but I didn't know much about them. Dinda knew Manzoni inside out, she had a pile of books. And I started to write. I would take bits to her, she would read them, and I would keep going, asking her for help at each stage.

GALLO She's a great teller of family stories, so a story about this extraordinary family had to be written by her and no one else, really.

SINIBALDI The "Things They Used to Say" of the Manzoni family.

GALLO Well, yes. Because everyone knows about Manzoni, but the family, less so. And she managed to bring these people to light in an extraordinary way.

GINZBURG The first thing I had read was *Giulia Beccaria*, which is a beautiful book by Donata Chiomenti Vassalli. I would like Einaudi to reprint it, and I hope one day they will. That was my starting point. Then Dinda gave me *Manzoni intimo, l'Epistolario* (Manzoni revealed: The letters). There was that. Dinda went with me to Brusuglio, to the library in Milan. We looked for copies of the letters. I knew all too well that I must never interpolate "Manzoni thought," "Manzoni said," never, because everything had to be taken from the letters. But as to these letters, sometimes I put too many of them in the book.

SINIBALDI That is, even Manzoni's "I" was missing.

GINZBURG There were no "I"s. It was in some way a book in the third person. At first I wanted to write about the women, but then these men came out.

SINIBALDI The women play a significant part in *The Manzoni Family*.

GINZBURG Yes. But then I came across Fauriel, a wonderful character, mysterious. And the stepson Stefano. These are the two men.

SINIBALDI *L'intervista* (The interview), your last play, has received some extraordinarily positive reactions from your harshest critics, from Garboli and your sons. Would it have anything to do with the fact that your playwriting has abandoned those lighter themes that Morante so disliked and has become instead more diagnostic, more profound in its analysis of the world today? "I Don't Like This World" was the title of an interview you gave to *Panorama* in '73 coinciding with the publication of the book *Dear Michael*. "I don't like this world"—what didn't you like? What were you starting to dislike in this world and in these times?

GINZBURG I like it even less now.

SINIBALDI That would have been my next question, but . . .

GINZBURG Yes. What didn't I like then?

SINIBALDI What was the reason?

GINZBURG The breakdown of families. It seems an affliction of our times. Not that families as they were before were so good. I think they were terrible. But I think people are now used to families breaking down, a kind of contagion. And this is too sad. I believe that a person needs a family—no matter how bad, repressive, disastrous—behind him. And the absence of this is making people grow up with problems. That's one thing. Then, in Italy the rural class is in decline, its culture, and that also seems really sad, something that shouldn't have happened. I was told off for saying this, both by Vittorio Foa and also by my brother, Gino Martinoli, when he said that people in rural areas were dying of malnutrition and of pellagra. I think we could have changed things so that they didn't die, so that they lived a better life. We could have made things better for these people, and kept them there. I think Italy has been industrialized badly and as a result we have lost a lot of important values. I think I'm right in thinking that this was what Pasolini thought as well.

SINIBALDI Yes, of course.

GINZBURG And this seems a great loss to me. They've built motorways where there were fields, meadows, and they've filled Italy with cars. Trains just don't work properly. I think this has affected everyone; it has created problems for people. The suburban housing projects are horrible beehives, and this has caused problems for the young and for people in general. A destructive process has been at

145

work in a country made for agriculture and for tourism. They wanted to make Italy into an industrialized country, and to me that's a mistake. But everyone says that I'm wrong.

SINIBALDI Not according to Pasolini, though.

GINZBURG I maintain still that malnutrition and pellagra can be eliminated. In not doing so, they have—

MASOLINO D'AMICO —eliminated a culture.

GINZBURG Eliminated a culture!

SINIBALDI Was there a particular moment when you became aware of this destruction, of a cultural collapse?

GINZBURG In the 1970s I was aware there was a general malaise, and I thought it came from that. There's also something in feminism that I don't like, I have to say, I who am a feminist as we all must be, men and women, fighting for the freedom of women. But feminism has created competitiveness, which I don't think is right. Women now have a winner mentality. And this means that women today feel a great sense of loneliness. Men don't know what part to play. Women know what part to play but they very much feel the lack of men. I think women need men just as men need women. And it's this I've tried to convey through my novels: the loneliness of women and the fragility of men.

SINIBALDI But don't you think that this characteristic, which you attribute to feminism, is just a sign of the times?

GINZBURG Yes, and ultimately it's right. Women were bound up in servitude, and they have to an extent freed themselves. Not everywhere, though. Freeing women from servitude seems sacrosanct to me. But what I mean is that there now exists a widespread inequality that is not right. Because even when women have the same rights as men, they also have more duties, and there is nothing you can do about this. That's how it is. Women just have a heavier burden, and no amount of feminism can free them. I think motherhood is more demanding than fatherhood, because the ties between a mother and her children are stronger. And this creates an enormous burden on women. This needs to be kept in mind.

MIRELLA FULVI And wasn't feminism a healthy reaction to what you call a "burden," so that we can better understand this situation?

GINZBURG Of course, it is a healthy reaction. But even healthy reactions can become distorted. There are feminist women whom I love and admire enormously: one is Livia Turco. But I can't see the world as she sees it: only according to a woman's dimension. It doesn't work for me; I think that the world must be seen from two angles, at once the men's and the women's.

SINIBALDI You don't believe in points of view that lean to one side? You don't believe that a degree of vindication—

GINZBURG No. When I see "women writers" it makes my skin crawl because I think there's no such thing as women writers.

FULVI But I think that . . . inevitably you have to go from a state in which you see your own reality from very close up in order to see it then from a well-rounded point of view.

GINZBURG This is what I'm told, that I'm ahead, that I'm one step ahead.

SINIBALDI In general you are reproached for being behind; so if for once they are accusing you of being too far ahead . . .

GINZBURG Actually, they accuse me of being behind the times because I'm conservative. To me, the business of equal rights is a given now and we must move on.

FULVI But you were saying that it isn't really a given.

GINZBURG It's true there are great, huge areas where women are still in a state of servitude. Still, my feeling is that women nowadays are generally free and strong, but they feel the lack of free and strong men, because men, on the other hand, are now mortified and weak. That's how it seems to me.

FULVI Because of women?

GINZBURG Not because of women, but a state of unease has developed between men and women that wasn't there before. Perhaps I'm mistaken, but that's how it seems to me.

SINIBALDI Yes, probably men are mortified because it's men who made history . . .

GINZBURG Now they don't know what role to play.

SINIBALDI And the stage we're at in history is a terrible one in many ways—if we think of the terrible ecological problems, how the planet is to survive—it is a male legacy.

GINZBURG Yes, of course.

SINIBALDI A historical mortification. It's a kind of historical defeat.

GINZBURG That's true.

SINIBALDI The relationship with the times in which one lives, is that a theme of all the books you've written? Is the theme of the breakdown of the family the point, the most sensitive knot of what seems to you to be a more general disintegration?

GINZBURG Absolutely.

147

SINIBALDI One of your texts, written in 1970, called *Collective Life*, is exemplary of your dissent from your times. But it is an almost maternal dissent as regards young people of the sixties and seventies.

GINZBURG Yes, of course, of course.

SINIBALDI Whom, as we shall see, you criticized deeply.

GINZBURG Well, in general, in the novels I've written, young people are positive. Fragile but positive. Both Michael and in *The City and the House*, they're fragile but positive.

SINIBALDI And there's also an allusion to the years that Pasolini referred to as the "anthropological revolution."

GINZBURG Yes.

SINIBALDI And it seems to me that in so far as the time frame is concerned, your analysis and Pasolini's coincide: it's the time of consumerism, the revolution that cut the history of Italy in two. Let's listen now to an extract from *Collective Life*:

> If I must be truthful, the time in which I live inspires me only with boredom and loathing. If it is because I have grown old and backward-looking, bored, and hypochondriacal or, if, on the other hand, what I feel is a justified loathing, I couldn't say. I think that many people of my generation are asking themselves just the same question.
>
> I have the impression that the boredom and loathing began in me at a specific moment. I couldn't say exactly when such a moment occurred, but I do know that it all happened suddenly and not bit by bit. It was a few years ago, perhaps five or six years ago. Before, everything that my contemporaries followed or loved was neither odious to me nor hard to understand; everything that intrigued, seduced, pulled in the people around me intrigued, seduced, and pulled me in as well. Whereas suddenly I felt that it wasn't so anymore, that I was still following inside of me things that people around me couldn't care less about, and vice versa. And the things that so delighted people like me filled me with repulsion. If I had to translate what happened to me into an image, I would say that it was as if the world suddenly became covered in mushrooms, and I'm not interested in these mushrooms.
>
> But I would like to understand if it is something that I should explain with my own, private, and personal old age or if, instead, a justified loathing has suddenly made its presence felt in me. Such an attitude of indifference or repulsion toward the things

that intrigue or appeal to others, toward habits that are going on around us in the present seems to me to be, frankly, the sign of a dull-witted and reprehensible approach. To refuse the present, to isolate oneself in regrets for a past that is now dead and gone, that means to refuse to think.

But even more dull-witted and even more worthy of reproach is the opposite approach: that is, to force ourselves to love and follow everything new around us. This is even more of an offence against truth. It means to be frightened of revealing ourselves to be who we are, that is, tired, bitter, by now old and immobile. It means to be terrified of being pushed to one side, to be terrified of being rejected, with our useless regrets in our ruined kingdoms.

That our regrets for a world dead and gone are useless goes without saying. In fact, that world, such as it was, will never be able to rise again. And it is questionable whether it was a world worthy of our regrets. The fact that we are inclined to regret its passing, having been the world that sheltered our youth, is indicative only of a sentimental tendency, a weakness of our spirit.

Having said that, however, it must also be said that it is totally impossible for man to establish what is useful and what is not useful to him. Man doesn't know.

149

I think that essentially what I hate about my time is in fact a false conception of what is useful and what is not. "Useful" is the term applied to science, technology, sociology, psychoanalysis, freedom from sexual taboos. All this is deemed useful, and people revere it. The rest is dismissed as useless. But among the rest is a world of things. They are necessarily classed as useless because they do not bring with them any palpable benefits to the destinies of the human race. To list them all would be difficult, as they are infinite. Among them is individual moral judgment, individual responsibility, individual moral conduct. Among them is the anticipation of death. Everything that constitutes the life of the individual. Among them is solitary thought, imagination and memory, regret for ages gone by, melancholia. Everything that makes up the life of poetry. A word such as this, neglected, spurned, and humiliated, seems today so ancient and sullied with old tears and dust, it is as if it is the very specter of uselessness, and one is almost embarrassed to use it.

Given that everything that goes to make up the life of the individual is then neglected and mortified, while the gods of collective existence are venerated and sanctified, the result is that solitary thought is no longer valued. It has been decreed that it serves no purpose, that it has no power, that it has no part to play in the life of the universe. With humanity seeming so diseased, the only things classed as useful are those that are believed to be capable of curing it.

Solitary thought seems to be nothing more than a melancholic and sterile fruit of solitude and hard work, and two things today are aggressively derided and put down: hard work and solitude. We try to fight them and annihilate them wherever we see even the smallest sign. We gather together in groups to defend ourselves from darkness and silence, from the tiring and draining presence of one's own single being. We gather together to travel, to exist, to play music, and sing, to create works of art. We even gather together to make love because the famous and most ancient rapport between one single woman and one single man seems too tiring and draining, too close to solitude.

The desire to defend oneself in any way possible from solitude and hard work is most apparent in two expressive outlets of today's life—in creative works and in the relationships between men and women.

SINIBALDI And that brings us back to the problem of relationships between men and women, which seems to be at the center, for you, of this transformation of our times. Are you nostalgic?

GINZBURG I have a great nostalgia for the nineteenth century. When I was writing The Manzoni Family, I was fascinated by the nineteenth century. That's not to forget that the Manzoni family is stricken with great misfortune, and the times in which they lived seem terrible. I do feel a nostalgia for the last century. It's a nostalgia without meaning, because when I think of the last century, I think of the life of the bourgeoisie, of the aristocracy. I don't think of the life of the proletariat, of the poor.

SINIBALDI Of the large majority of the population.

GINZBURG Yes, I think of those who had lovely gardens, houses, armchairs, curtains, that's who I think of, not of the other part.

SINIBALDI Well, you must admit that you can't feel nostalgia for the other part, surely?

GINZBURG Of course not . . . It's a feeling, a wrong one, but I must own up to it.

SINIBALDI You are currently actively involved in politics, in a parliamentary role. Can we talk in terms of "commitment"? Do you see this term, which is often used to describe the relationship between intellectuals and society, as adequate to your activity?

GINZBURG The terms "commitment" and its opposite, "disengagement," were constantly being used in the postwar period. At a certain point I thought I wanted disengagement . . . not that I wanted it, but that it was indispensable for a novelist. That a novelist shouldn't set himself the task of trying to bring about improvements to society, but just stick to writing novels. I've never written novels that were committed; the idea of disengagement at a certain time seemed to me the only right one for a novelist. It's just that because I'm a person, like all people I am sensitive to the calls of a commitment to society. That is, I'm a novelist when I'm writing novels, but when I'm not writing them, I'm not. And then I feel the call to commitment to society. I must say that since being in Parliament I feel this much more often. I think that novels talk about society, life as it is, and they love it as it is. Intellectuals are those who want to comment on it and, perhaps, try to improve it. I think I am a novelist from head to toe. Sometimes, I'm not sure I'm exactly an intellectual, but something similar.

SINIBALDI Yes, because the stances you take don't bear much resemblance to the ones taken by intellectuals. For instance, they are distinguished by commitment to specific issues; it always seems as if there is something that at a certain point tramples on your sensitivity or provokes your indignation.

GINZBURG That's true, yes. And yet I did write the book about Serena Cruz. I wouldn't have written it if I hadn't been a member of Parliament.

SINIBALDI Because being a member of Parliament means you feel a particular responsibility?

GINZBURG No, it isn't that (I should, but it isn't that). I'm not a good member of Parliament; but I do feel more strongly that we must fight against injustice. I as a person tend to feel injustice but won't do anything about it; whereas since becoming a member of Parliament I have felt that I must make my voice heard and try to . . .

SINIBALDI It's a commitment that you show not only in the stances you take in public life but also in your work, as an editor. Anne Frank's *Diary* is the key book (or, at least, it's the most popular book: it has sold sixteen million copies around the world) about the Jewish tragedy in the concentration camps. It is a book that is only now being published in its complete edition in Holland and Germany, so people will have the whole picture of this extraordinary girl. How did you discover this book?

GINZBURG Well, it arrived . . . I was in Turin, I was working at Einaudi, a copy of this book arrived. I read it along with Paolo Serini, who was a consultant. And that's it, we had it translated from the Dutch—I read it in French—and had it published.

SINIBALDI It was published for the first time in '54, or before even?

GINZBURG I think before, but I can't say when for sure. I must have read it . . . I was in Turin, so I must have read it in 1950 or '49.

SINIBALDI In an interview that came out this week in *Rinascita*, which was in response to events that began at Carpentras[1] and, therefore, to the alarming resurgence, in a ferocious form, of antiSemitism, among the few possible therapies, you suggested this: get people to read Anne Frank's *Diary*, get people to read Primo Levi's books, get people to see films, to make them remember.

GINZBURG Yes. Get them to remember, it's so important, essential.

SINIBALDI And do you think it will be enough?

GINZBURG No, but it is something that should be done to ensure that in schools children are aware of what happened to Jews in those years, what genocide was.

SINIBALDI Because your impression is that people forget, that there's a tendency to forget?

GINZBURG People claimed that Anne Frank's *Diary* was a fake, that it was written as part of pro-Jewish propaganda. They said awful things.

SINIBALDI In fact, along with the appearance of the complete Anne Frank's *Diary*, we've seen reports published by those who knew her in the camp, who saw her die, resolving any doubts.

GINZBURG Yes. Did you read that book based on the descriptions by one of her peers, someone who met her in the last days of her life?

SINIBALDI The tragedy of Anne Frank unites two themes—that of the Jews and that of children. Your presence regarding these issues has been a strong one, a call that couldn't be ignored. Do you agree?

GINZBURG I think I thought a lot during the period of persecution about my children. We suffered persecution; I was afraid they would take them away from me during '43–'44.

SINIBALDI So two intertwined conditions, the one of the Jews and the one of children?

GINZBURG Yes.

SINIBALDI An essay of yours, written in 1972 (we will hear an extract from it) has a precise and burning subject matter, and a short, striking title, "The Jews." It is a text that came out, I think, in *La Stampa*. In '72 right after the [Munich] massacre.[2]

GINZBURG I received threatening letters from all sides over this text.

SINIBALDI For that text you were accused of being both pro-Jewish and anti-Semitic.

GINZBURG Yes.

SINIBALDI This is an example of just how this particular sensitivity can sometimes seem to be yours alone; it leads you into conflict with all types of people. I don't know if this is your impression, but . . .

GINZBURG Yes, that's how I see it.

SINIBALDI Let's listen to "The Jews."

Everything that regards Jews always seems to involve me directly. I'm only part Jewish, on my father's side, but I've always thought that my Jewish side must be heavier and more burdensome in me than my other side. If I happen to meet someone somewhere who I discover is Jewish, instinctively I feel that I have an affinity with that person. After a minute I may find him or her unbearable, but there stays in me a sense of secret complicity. This is a side of my nature that I find strange and that I don't like at all, because it is openly at odds with everything that I have thought over the course of my life, because I maintain that there are no affinities, except for extremely superficial ones, between Jews, because I think that men must go beyond the confines of their origins. That is what I think, but when I meet a Jew I can't help but feel a strange and dark sensation of connivance.

When I heard about the massacre [in Munich], I thought that they had killed yet again those of my blood. I thought this in the midst of a sea of other thoughts, but I thought it. In thinking it, I felt disgusted with myself because it was a feeling worthy of disgust. I don't believe at all that Jews have a different blood than other people. I don't believe there exists divisions through blood.

I'm Jewish and I've had a bourgeois upbringing. This bourgeois upbringing has instilled in me some false ideas. I must have somehow breathed in, during childhood, the idea that Jews and the bourgeoisie had rights and superiority over others. No such thing has ever been said to me in my house, and in fact, I was always

153

taught that all men have equal rights. But in the structure of my upbringing there must have been an idea of superiority. We spend our lives struggling to free ourselves from the vices of our upbringing, but the vices of our upbringing remain imprinted on our spirit like tattoos. In our adult life, we spend our time cleansing our spirit of these tattoos.

As for the Jews of Israel, I think I thought that they had rights and superiority over the Arabs. At a certain moment this seemed a monstrous idea. I pulled it out of me and trampled on it furiously. But I realized that I had cultivated such a monstrous idea in me over many years, like a plant on the windowsill. So even though I pulled it out and trampled on it, I'm not absolutely sure that there aren't still shreds of it in me. Our monstrous ideas have the ability to make us understand the make-up of our interior landscape. A monstrous idea happily grows and proliferates there without making anything around it disappear. It grows and proliferates next to our better impulses and our thirst for justice and equality, without making them disappear but transforming them ever so slowly into a pile of rotten straw.

Our monstrous ideas should also have the ability to make us understand our enemies or those whom we are accustomed to calling our enemies. They should teach us to rest our gaze on others with tolerance and very close attention. After we have pulled them out and trampled on them, we should hold onto their memory and stop thinking of ourselves as the children of the universal good.

At times I have thought that the Jews of Israel had rights and superiority over others because they had survived an extermination campaign. This wasn't a monstrous idea, but it was a mistake. The pain and massacre of innocents that we have watched and shared in over our lifetime, this does not give us any right over others or any kind of superiority. Those who have known personally the burden of fears have no right to oppress those so similar to them with money or arms, simply because no living soul in the world has this right.

With regard to the Jews of Israel, this is what happens to me. If someone speaks against them I feel rebellious and secretly offended. It is as if my own family is being offended. But if someone speaks of them with admiration and devotion, I have the immediate sensation that I do not share these feelings either and that I am on the other side.

After the war, we loved and felt compassion for the Jews who went to Israel, thinking that they had survived an attempt to exterminate them, that they were homeless and didn't know where to go. We loved in them the memories of pain, the fragility, the aimless walk and the shoulders oppressed by fears. These are traits that we love today in man. We were not at all prepared to see them become a powerful nation, aggressive and vengeful. We hoped that they would be a small unarmed country, peace-loving, that each of them would keep their own fragile, bitter, reflective and solitary physiognomy. Perhaps that wasn't possible. But this transformation is one of the horrible things that has occurred.

When someone speaks of Israel with admiration, I feel as if I'm on the other side. I understood at a certain point, perhaps late, that the Arabs were poor farmers and shepherds. I know very few things about myself, but I do know with absolute certainty that I don't want to be on the side of those who use arms, money, and culture to oppress farmers and shepherds.

Our instinct pushes us to be on one side or the other. But in truth, nowadays it is impossible to be on one side or the other. Men and whole peoples undergo such rapid and horrible transformations. The only choice open to us is to be on the side of those who are unfairly dying or suffering. People will say that this is an easy choice, but perhaps it is the only choice that today is left open to us.

SINIBALDI These harsh and certainly complex comment on Jews came out at a dramatic moment for the state of Israel. That is, in the days following the massacre of Israeli athletes by Palestinian guerrillas in [Munich]. Your comment met with harsh reactions.

GINZBURG Yes. I got so many indignant letters—some agreeing, but most indignant—from Jews, and also indignant ones from anti-Semitic non-Jews. So, I got a lot of letters.

SINIBALDI And you haven't changed your mind?

GINZBURG No.

SINIBALDI Not at all, over these last twenty years, and with everything that has transpired?

GINZBURG No, I haven't changed my mind. The conflict between Israel and the Palestinians is simply one more hardship that has befallen us. It seems to be one of the most painful lacerations from which we suffer.

SINIBALDI But don't you think that this dream, mentioned here, of a small, unarmed and peace-loving state is even further off now?

GINZBURG Oh, yes, of course, but that's what it should have been. I have never been a Zionist. Leone Ginzburg was not a Zionist—perhaps I've already told you that. I've never been a Zionist. Maybe if there had been the possibility of giving them a land that was for them alone and that did not already belong to others, in Canada or I don't know where.

SINIBALDI This is, in your opinion, the original sin of the Middle East question?

GINZBURG Yes . . . yes. That the Jews had been chased out of their countries, had seen their houses destroyed and their lives destroyed, and we understand that they were seeking a refuge; that is totally understandable. But the mistake was for them to create an armed state: I think this was truly a terrible mistake. And now we find ourselves with the Shamir government, which is a horrendous government.

SINIBALDI You had a Jewish father and a Catholic mother, and have often alluded to your basic extraneousness, when you were a girl, to these religions, together with all that belonging to a religion meant, at that time in particular . . . that is, a social identity . . .

GINZBURG Yes. I feel Jewish and Catholic, both. I don't know how, I couldn't explain it. I don't love priests as a rule, but I do feel great fondness for a few of them. There are priests who seem extraordinary to me, the ones we read about these days in the papers. I won't mention names here, but . . .

SINIBALDI It's easy to guess whom you mean: priests who are in the front line in some of the battles that you also feel strongly about.

GINZBURG Well, yes, of course. I feel profoundly Jewish because Jews have been exterminated. I felt at that time just how much Jewishness there was in me. I also felt Catholic. I couldn't explain it.

SINIBALDI In keeping with the discussion, I would like for you to recall the figure of Primo Levi, your friend for many years.

GINZBURG Yes.

SINIBALDI With whom you exchanged many opinions.

GINZBURG Not so many. He saw a lot of one of my brothers, in '47. I didn't know him; he was close to my brother Alberto, who was a doctor. They saw each other often, and I would sometimes see him at his house. But we weren't exactly friends then. Then we began to exchange a few ideas. He had a few reservations about this article, "The Jews." He agreed up to a point but also had some reservations.

SINIBALDI Were you badly affected by his tragic death?

GINZBURG Yes, very much so. But I think that every suicide has a thousand causes, a thousand origins, a thousand motivations. I think that in him the memories of the Nazi camps never went away, and at a certain time it became so painful as to be unbearable. Lots of people have killed themselves after coming back from concentration camps: there's Celan, and Bettelheim. And there's that friend of Primo Levi's called Améry.[3]

SINIBALDI Ah, yes. His books have been published in Italy just recently.

GINZBURG Améry wrote that lovely book *At the Mind's Limits*. I think it's not so much, as people have said, the sense of guilt for having survived: not so much this, but simply the diabolical memories of those camps.

SINIBALDI Now we have a particular piece for you to hear. It's the voice of Primo Levi, from a radio broadcast, "The Sky Is a Mirror," which was broadcast in January 1985.[4] Primo Levi talks about reactions to the book *If This Is a Man*, from '47. It is his most famous book, in which he wrote most directly and in the most uncompromising way about the tragic experience of the death camps:

157

PRIMO LEVI I receive almost every week two or three readers' letters, mostly young readers, who ask me questions that are always the same.

ALBERTO GOZZI What do they ask you?

PRIMO LEVI They ask eight things, I don't know if I can remember them all now. The first, which is never missing, is why this book that denounces atrocious actions on the part of a considerable percentage of the German population against the Jewish people contains no hatred.

ALBERTO GOZZI How do you answer this first question?

PRIMO LEVI With difficulty. I don't know why, but I am physiologically incapable of hating. It's a thing that I don't know, like I don't know anger, it isn't a state of mind to which I am prone. I've felt anger very few times in my life, hatred almost never, which doesn't mean that I don't feel and didn't feel then and still feel to this day an overwhelming need for justice. If I were a judge I wouldn't hesitate to condemn in an extremely severe way, and often to death, some of these people. I was satisfied by Eichmann's death sentence, it seemed disputable from a legal point of view even if I'm not a legal expert, but, as a man, it satisfied me on a human level, even though I can't say that I hated even Eichmann. Faced with the figure of Eichmann, as with many others, all the ones from Nuremberg who were condemned, my first reaction is not hatred but, rather, curiosity. This may come as a surprise; perhaps it is part of my training as a technician, a chemist: I would like and I do like to go and look inside things but also inside people. From then, a "naturalistic" interest of mine, like someone who studies an insect or a bird, is turned toward those on the other side, not necessarily Nazis. I'm keen to understand; I become addicted, in fact, to reading these things, the biographies of the people on the other side. Not necessarily Nazis. In the same way I'm interested in man and anti-man, that is, what has become perverted or people have let become perverted, which perverts.

ALBERTO GOZZI Does perversion, monstrosity manage to be as total as it seems to us and to your younger readers?

PRIMO LEVI No, and in fact there is no such thing. I would say that the result of this research of mine—which is not systematic but sporadic (and which was done also via research which others have carried out and via my own observations, since during and after I have come into contact with such people)—is that there is no monster. Or at least, it is extremely rare, I have never seen one. The surprise in this research is that they are people like us, but they have taken, they have been channeled along a road that perverts, which is the road of abdication from moral law, and also from reason, because for the most part they are all people who have made the wrong calculations. Beyond guilt, sin (I say this even though I am not religious) there is also a mistake, a miscalculation. They thought for the most part that they would gain advantages that they didn't in fact gain.

SIX

FAMILY AND BORGHESIA

MARINO SINIBALDI Let's listen to an excerpt from *The Little Virtues* [discussed above] entitled "Il mio mestiere" (My Vocation). Together with other extracts we've heard each of these four Sundays in May, it helps us put together a kind of collage of Natalia Ginzburg's vocation and activity as a writer.

After the time when I lived in the South I got to know grief very well—a real, irremediable and incurable grief that shattered my life, and when I tried to put it together again I realized that I and my life had become something irreconcilable with what had gone before. Only my vocation remained unchanged—the tools were still the same, but the way I used them had changed. At first I hated it, it disgusted me, but I knew very well that I would end up returning to it and that it would save me. Sometimes I would think that I had not been so unfortunate in my life and that I was unjust when I accused destiny of never having shown me any kindness, because it had given me my three children and my vocation. Besides, I could not imagine my life without my vocation. It was always there, it had never left me for a moment, and when I believed that it slept, its vigilant, shining eyes were still watching me.

Such is my vocation. It does not produce much money, and it is always necessary to follow some other vocation simultaneously in order to live. Although sometimes it produces a little and it is very satisfying to have money because of it—it is like receiving money and presents from the hands of someone you love. Such is my vocation. I do not, I repeat, know much about the value of the results it has given me or could give me: or it would be better to say that I know the relative though certainly not the absolute value of the results I have already obtained. When I write something I usually think it is very important and that I am a very fine writer. I think this happens to everyone. But there is one corner of my mind in which I know very well what I am, which is a small, a very small writer. I swear I know it. But that doesn't matter much to me. Only, I don't want to think about names: I can see that if I am asked "a small writer like who?" it would sadden me to think of the names of other small writers. I prefer to think that no one has ever been like me, however small, however much a mosquito or a flea of a writer I may be. The important thing is to be convinced that this really is your vocation, your profession, something you will do all your life. But as a vocation it is no joke. There are innumerable dangers besides those I have mentioned. We are constantly threatened with grave dangers whenever we write a page. There is the danger of suddenly starting to be flirtatious and of singing. I always have a crazy desire to sing, and I have to be very careful that I don't. And there is the danger of cheating with words that do not really exist within us, that we have picked up by chance from outside of ourselves and that we skillfully slip in because we have become a bit dishonest. There is the danger of cheating and being dishonest. As you see, it is quite a difficult vocation, but it is the finest one in the world. The days and houses of our life, the days and houses of the people with whom we are involved, books and images and thoughts and conversations—all these things feed it, and it grows within us. It is a vocation that also feeds on terrible things, it swallows the best and the worst in our lives, and our evil feelings flow in its blood just as much as our benevolent feelings. It feeds itself and grows within us.[1]

SINIBALDI This text is from '49 when it appeared in Il Ponte. We have been using it over the last few weeks as if it were a contemporary text. Do you have something to add?

NATALIA GINZBURG No, no, I wouldn't want to change anything. Well, perhaps I wouldn't use the word "vocation" now. It doesn't really fit . . .

SINIBALDI Here with us is Enzo Siciliano. [*To Enzo Siciliano*] At the start of the seventies in the review *Paragone* writing about *Never Must You Ask Me*, you said, "Natalia Ginzburg is a writer you either love or hate."

ENZO SICILIANO Well, because *Never Must You Ask Me* is a bundle of articles that whipped up a kind of storm in the newspaper when they were published; and there were people who were for Natalia and people who were against her. You see, Natalia has a very peremptory and direct way of exposing her own thoughts. This way she has of being direct, it's a way that divides the field. Because it is very difficult for anyone, and especially for a writer (but perhaps also for an Italian writer), to perceive how reality is unfolding with the direct and clear vision that Natalia has. It's a gift; it's a nature. Very few people have it; it's her character to be, as it were, inside a book, inside a page, inside a phrase. There's something extremely naked and pure about the way in which Natalia exposes herself and narrates a situation. And the reader either goes along with it or, if he is used to another type of attitude, he opts out. That's when the storm starts. That's how it is. Natalia represents—as far as Italian literature and narrative of the second half of the twentieth century goes—an unusual and almost unique case.

SINIBALDI Why unique?

SICILIANO Because of her ability to get to things without intellectual filters. I can't think of many writers, even important ones, who can do this. In terms of the nature of feelings and passions, a poet like Penna had it and still does. But writers with this immediacy and this strength of impact, I can't think of anyone other than Natalia.

SINIBALDI Right. And for you, Natalia Ginzburg, this expression, "You either love her or hate her," what impression did that have on you? Do you have the impression of being loved or hated by readers?—I mean as a writer, not as a person . . .

GINZBURG I do have that sensation. I've always had it.

SINIBALDI It doesn't bother you?

GINZBURG To be hated does bother me, but I think that's how it must be.

SINIBALDI It's a price you pay, in some way.

GINZBURG Yes, perhaps because, as I've already said, I haven't a

163

cultural background, and that bothers me. I've never managed to be cultured.

SICILIANO But that's not true, you put yourself down, Natalia!

GINZBURG No, I'm not putting myself down.

SICILIANO Yes, you are!

GINZBURG No, I've never been very cultured; it's something I lack. I wasn't good at school; I think it came from there. And then I've never really tried to develop a cultural background. My husband Gabriele Baldini was an enormously cultivated man, and I could sense how much I was missing. He knew everything I don't know. I would go to the cinema, I loved it, but then I couldn't remember the names in a film, so it didn't become part of my cultural memory. Gabriele had an enormous awareness of cinema, and he knew languages, which I didn't. He knew about music, and I don't. He knew about painting. He had a huge cultural background, and I have always keenly felt the lack of one.

SINIBALDI Cesare Garboli, in his introduction to the Meridiani edition of your works, says that he always saw in these kinds of statements a break with a universe or a culture that was predominantly masculine. And he saw this as a form of isolation or rebellion.

SICILIANO Well I'm not sure of this, no . . . Perhaps Garboli has a very vivid psychological perception, but I'm not sure Natalia's attitude is born out of rebellion. I think when she talks of her husband Gabriele's "cultural background," she means that when presented with this vastness she felt, and still feels, diminished.

GINZBURG Yes . . . diminished. It's not that it gave me an inferiority complex, but I felt that I had to trot along on my own account, that I had to do it my own way. And I have often been criticized, because, in general, when I talk about cinema I say, "But I don't understand cinema," when I talk about painting I say, "I don't know much about it." But it's just that I want to say so right off the bat, because it's better that they don't believe I know things I don't.

SICILIANO You hit the nail on the head when you said, "I have to do it my way." But your way is brilliant, and that's the point. Plus, I think great cultural learning is useful only up to a point. If you have a certain nature, that kind of equipment is useful; if you don't have a certain nature, it's no use at all.

GINZBURG Yes, yes, I agree.

SICILIANO You see? No, what you have instead is a capacity to react, to understand the nucleus of truth or reality contained in each event, and to talk about it.

SINIBALDI And that is true of both your narrative texts and your articles and of your polemical or political writings.

SICILIANO Yes.

GINZBURG And narrative. Yes, because I feel like I'm moving through a world that I hardly know.

SINIBALDI Garboli didn't exactly speak in terms of rebellion; he said that there is a regime of "indifference" and "sleepiness" in Ginzburg as regards male intellectual domains. That's not exactly rebellion.

GINZBURG Because I never had a real inferiority complex. When I was young I hoped to create for myself this cultural background, but then it never happened, and at a certain time I resigned myself to the fact.

SINIBALDI And this seems an extraneousness in some way—to lead us back to a theme that opened today's discussion—an extraneousness from a male intellectual apparatus.

SICILIANO But I can't make this distinction between male and female writers.

SINIBALDI Which is just what Natalia Ginzburg has said today.

SICILIANO I can't do that. When I read any text the sex is out of the picture.

GINZBURG Yes, you have to try to be neither man nor woman when you talk to men and women: try to be neither one thing nor the other. But a woman takes with her a woman's physiognomy, that's for sure. [2] Just as Svevo always wrote out of the fact that he was from Trieste but still wrote something that was for everyone . . . I think the same goes for women as far as regards men.

SINIBALDI I would like now to talk a little about Ginzburg's later works—at least, the narrative ones, the two long stories "Family" and "Borghesia," which were published together in '77, and then the last novel, *The City and the House,* from '84. I think it should be Enzo Siciliano who talks about these, because they were defined by Garboli as Natalia Ginzburg's "Roman novels," as was *Dear Michael.* But also because these texts seemed to bring out those extreme love/hate reactions to her work . . . do you agree?

SICILIANO In the two long stories, "Family" and *The City and the House,* Natalia had—how can I put it—plundered her own style and her capacities as a storyteller to achieve a linearity, a tragic purity. And the same goes for the way she wrote: the language, the design of the characters, and the way in which they connect with one another. Everything is extremely linear and simple, and yet in this simplicity she manages to recover a mass of emotions, a complexity of emotions such as we find in the world today. It isn't easy to describe it: the narrative apparatus, the style that Natalia has. It's horizontal, linear. She uses broken phrasing that doesn't allow for sudden spirals upward or inward. Her language is highly communicative, totally unadorned, and never panders to the reader. Faced with the complexity of today's existence, all this becomes extremely transparent. But the fact is Natalia writes about things she knows. Like every authentic narrator, she doesn't consciously set out to photograph life, to represent it, to map it sociologically. Her work represents the dream of the life that she lives every day: perhaps to spread the load of it, to disempower it or to empower it even more. Or perhaps simply to keep a record of it, not to let it turn to ashes.

GINZBURG I agree.

SICILIANO I think this is what she wants to do, and she does it with extraordinary faithfulness to what she feels, to what she sees. And in this way—

SINIBALDI —in this way she also reaches a sociological precision?

SICILIANO But the recognition of that comes later. It's up to certain readers to figure out.

SINIBALDI Are you referring to the disintegration of the bourgeois family? Which is a small, but not so small, phenomenon.

SICILIANO That's exactly it. But it's the reader's job to connect the dots. We must keep in mind that a narrator's job is not to make himself complex in relation to the reality that he wants to represent, but to represent reality for how it is represented. To narrate to himself this dream of living, which readers can then recover however they want, even in a sociological way. But if you want to understand Natalia . . . [*To Ginzburg*] You recently wrote something that was not a self-portrait but, rather, a portrait of a great writer whom you've always loved . . . Chekhov, am I right?

GINZBURG Yes.

SICILIANO You seem to regard him as a kind of light shining in the darkness. Each one of us has such a light, be we writers or not—we have what Baudelaire referred to as "beacons."

GINZBURG Yes, yes.

SINIBALDI Another aspect of Natalia's work that divides people is her writing for the theater. I would like to discuss her plays with the help of Guido Fink, who is on the phone now. Hello, Guido Fink!

GUIDO FINK Hello.

SINIBALDI In 1971 you published an article in Il Mondo about Ginzburg's La porta sbagliata (The wrong door).

FINK Yes.

SINIBALDI You say that, "Behind the delicacy of her touch, the battle that Ginzburg leads in the theater and in her writing for the theater is brave and extremely tough." In fact, that article had a steely title: "Valiant Ginzburg."

FINK That was the editor's choice!

SINIBALDI The editor's choice. You say, "All the more (brave and tough) for the fact that she is aware of the inevitability of defeat." Well, we know that Natalia Ginzburg is not turned back by the word "defeat."

GINZBURG Not at all.

SINIBALDI She is more inclined to hate victories.

GINZBURG Yes, absolutely.

SINIBALDI So, this harsh assessment, where did it come from? Where did you get this impression of a way of writing for theater that was knowingly headed for defeat? We're not talking, of course, about creative failure . . .

FINK Well, I don't know exactly what I meant at the time, but neither do I want to adapt what I said in light of Garboli's idea of "toughness." However, it seems to me—and it has been confirmed in previous programs—that Natalia's need to write plays partly serves as a filter; it allows the writer to flee the fear of the pronoun "I" and to avoid writing literary fiction. The playwriting was a way for Ginzburg to throw away this great love of the written word. And in fact, I don't entirely agree with what Enzo Siciliano was saying a while ago when he spoke of Natalia Ginzburg as being a direct writer, a writer without filters. And neither, if I may say so, do I entirely agree with Natalia Ginzburg when she says, "I must be careful . . . I must trot along." Yes, but look how she trots along. Playwriting, along with the short epistolary novel Dear Michael, involved strategies of dissimulation just so she could create filters. Perhaps she was avoiding the long novel, the complicated plot, with all the requisite connections; because the truth is that a play like La segretaria (The secretary) or a novel like Dear Michael could have been done as great tragedies, great melodramas. The Manzoni Family was that, but it was all broken up, wasn't it? Everything somehow seemed tossed off. Same goes for Natalia's love of the word, which, in my opinion, embodies great stylistic wisdom. This happens also in the articles and essays being discussed today: what hides behind a seemingly humble thought is effectively a great moral conscience. And in the plays—I Married You for the Fun of It could be an Oscar Wilde comedy, where even the boring mothers-in-law and the empty-headed maids talk in such an appealing and entertaining way. And yet the play doesn't advertise Ginzburg's great talent, her supreme skill and wisdom. L'intervista (The interview) is wonderful as well. It isn't like her early plays where she creates a kind of refuge, a wall to protect her from time, history, changes . . . from the novel itself. Here years go by between one act and the next, there's this slow decline of an invisible character: there's everything that Ginzburg had perhaps avoided so far.

SICILIANO But there's also a story. Even in I Married You for the Fun of It or in La segretaria (The secretary), an entire past effectively becomes a novel at the moment it is spoken about on the stage. Or rather, the scene lives out the conflict in the characters precisely because behind them they've got a memory that is in some way novelistic, complex. I'm not sure I agree that Natalia's plays are born out of an abandonment of or diffidence toward the novel.

FINK A kind of hesitation.

SICILIANO Right. But it seems to me that the novel, as narrated complexity of existence, has always been there in her playwriting. Of course L'Intervista unfolds within a structure that she never used before: that is, you are aware of time, which is a more obviously novelistic trait.

GINZBURG Can I say something? It gave me great pleasure in that play to make ten years go by. It gave me great joy.

SINIBALDI In L'intervista? Which is the last one.

GINZBURG Which is the last play, yes.

SINIBALDI Which has just been published in the Collezione di Teatro (Play collection) series put out by Einaudi. Let's remember that it has a different structure. It no longer has a unity . . .

GINZBURG There are two characters instead of one, and they, a man and a woman, each perform a long monologue.

SINIBALDI And what strikes you, especially those who know Ginzburg's plays—and as Guido Fink very astutely commented—is the passing of time from one act to the next, from one scene to the next.

SICILIANO And then there's an absent protagonist . . .

FINK You could say that there's always been an absent protagonist, because how does I Married You for the Fun of It start? We are at the funeral of this Lamberto Genova, who was perhaps one sort of guy, perhaps another, maybe a psychoanalyst, maybe not. He was possibly the one who could explain this mystery, this talk that was spreading and that no longer had any meaning. This great divorce between words and things, which is there in a comic sense in I Married You for the Fun of It but in a much more melancholic sense in Dear Michael, don't you think? The absent person is Michael himself, isn't he?

GINZBURG Yes.

SICILIANO Yes, of course.

FINK Like a pure name, a pure absence. It's always been that way. And this maybe confirms what I was trying to say: how Natalia Ginzburg has always tried to cover something up. To cover something that is perhaps herself as author, as she was saying in the first part of this program. Hence I don't see any big difference, as far as playwriting or creativity in the strictest sense goes. I see, basically, this whole series of filters and masks, which aren't necessarily a negative feature . . . it's more a quality, which is one of the reasons I could never hate her.

[Laughter]

GINZBURG Thank you very much. The truth is I wrote plays to use the first person in a different form, using it to bring in so many people together, men, women. That is, using it in a way that was not autobiographical.

SINIBALDI Free.

GINZBURG Free. That's it. I use the first person because I don't know how to use the third person. I will never use the true third person, that is, the one found in someone who is looking down from above and saying what this person is thinking and what that one is thinking.

FINK Not even the journalistic "we"? When "we" is also an "I."

GINZBURG Well, yes, of course.

SINIBALDI I'd like to thank Guido Fink, who has been very kind and helped us a great deal.

GINZBURG Thank-you very much, thanks so much. 'Bye.

SINIBALDI I'd like to close this discussion dedicated to Ginzburg's writing by listening to a short piece of music connected to one of the very few instances when Natalia Ginzburg has spoken explicitly about music. The text, "Silence," was written in Turin and published, I think, in Felice Balbo's review in Cultura e realtà, in '51.

GINZBURG Yes, that's right.

SINIBALDI It's now included in the collection *The Little Virtues*, and it's an astute observation on one of the world's ills, the unease at the end of conversation, "incommunicability," as it has been termed in a more banal way. This text took as its point of departure Debussy's opera *Pelléas et Mélisande*.

[Music]

SINIBALDI This was the first scene of the fourth act, which inspired you to write the piece on silence that we mentioned. You said that, for you, a way of coming out of silence had been to go through psychoanalysis. Now, given that psychoanalysts appear every now and then (in a strange way) in your work . . . given that one of your best-known narrative essays is "La mia psicanalisi" (My psychoanalysis), what do you think of psychoanalysis? What was its value as far as your literary output was concerned? Do you want to tell us, because it is a famous story, for anyone who has read *Never Must You Ask Me* . . . the one about your psychoanalysis?

GINZBURG Yes.

SINIBALDI So, what was its importance? Your discovery of it came very early compared with the rest of Italian society. I remember something along similar lines in *Voices in the Evening*, where there's a homeopath at a time when few people knew about homeopathy.

GINZBURG Well, people talked about psychoanalysis. When I wrote that piece I had already been psychoanalyzed. For three months . . . not very long.

SINIBALDI A lightening quick analysis!

GINZBURG An extremely quick psychoanalysis. But I didn't mean that the character got better through silence; but it was one of the means by . . .

SINIBALDI No, it wasn't a cure; in fact, you described it in quite a cold way, like a kind of mechanical reaction to the silence, by talking continuously.

GINZBURG Yes, mechanical: talking to someone who is paid to listen to you.

SINIBALDI Let's move on now to another subject, Natalia and children. What springs to mind immediately is the case of Serena Cruz. "Children" was the title of your first story to be reviewed—the second one you ever wrote, at seventeen years old.

GINZBURG Yes, yes.

SINIBALDI And you pay very keen attention to pedagogic issues in various books. In *The Little Virtues*, the title comes from an essay about bringing up children. In fact, it's an essay that has such a beautiful beginning I would like to read it:

> As far as the education of children is concerned I think they should be taught not the little virtues but the great ones. Not thrift, but generosity and an indifference to money; not caution, but courage and a contempt for danger; not shrewdness, but frankness and a love of truth; not diplomacy, but love for one's neighbor and self-denial; not a desire for success, but a desire to be and to know.
>
> Usually we do just the opposite; we rush to teach them a respect for the little virtues . . .

So, did you feel this pedagogic vocation?

GINZBURG I felt it in so far as I tried to bring up my own children as best I could. It's extremely difficult to raise children right, almost impossible; you always make mistakes. But I had in my mind when I was bringing them up, that they had to be taught the greater virtues, not just the smaller ones.

SINIBALDI Generosity—perhaps this is the greater virtue that would sum up the rest.

GINZBURG Absolutely.

SINIBALDI As for Anne Frank's *Diary*, which you were the first at Einaudi to read, in French, and which marks the start of a sustained attention to the Jewish question, Hebraism, it's intriguing to retrace this interest and this sensitivity, this commitment to children.

GINZBURG Perhaps because during childhood I thought a lot about myself.

SINIBALDI As the youngest daughter, you had the right to see things generally from a child's perspective, perhaps?

GINZBURG And then I had children of my own, and as a result children have always been on my mind.

SINIBALDI Do you still observe them a lot?

GINZBURG I don't know if I observe them. At least, I'm not aware of doing so; but if there's a child present, I notice him. For example, I remember that when I was a small girl, they would give me adult books to read because they didn't have anything else; and I found them boring, but to get through them and to get more out of them, I would imagine there was a child in the story when actually there wasn't.

SINIBALDI You mean you rewrote novels in your head?

171

GINZBURG I would add a child who was absolutely not there. That made life more interesting.

SINIBALDI I would like now to listen to a story somewhat analogous to Anne Frank's story. It's a child's story, a tragic one. Natalia Ginzburg was the editor and translator for both works. It is *The Stones Cry Out: A Cambodian Childhood, 1975–1980*, a terrifying and extraordinary text about a historical tragedy that is still semi-unknown, unfortunately, or semi-removed, largely forgotten: the story of the three years of terror in Cambodia under the iron hand of Pol Pot, correct?

GINZBURG Yes, I was sent this book by Einaudi, the publishing house, by chance. And after I read it, I asked them to publish it, and I asked to translate it from the French.

SINIBALDI You're very attached to this book, aren't you?

GINZBURG I found it very moving. It's a frightening book, terrible. I really hadn't ever thought much about Cambodia, and so I started to follow this story, which is a dreadful one.

SINIBALDI And so far without an end . . . [3]

GINZBURG Yes, and this Pol Pot—

SINIBALDI He's still alive.

GINZBURG —and doing very well. Nobody's ever touched so much as a hair on his head.[4]

SINIBALDI He's still running his guerilla campaign with the support of Washington and Beijing.

GINZBURG Yes, having killed three million people.

SINIBALDI Let's listen to an excerpt from *The Stones Cry Out*. It's the opening, where nothing too awful happens (whereas the book as a whole is one long account of atrocities). But in the book, in the way the Khmer come into the city there's already a hint, as in a great novel, of the horror and the terror that is to come:

The war had been raging out in the countryside for a long time, but during the last two years, in particular, peasants had been streaming into the city, passing by our neighborhood, Tuol Svay Prey, not far from the sports stadium. My parents had long forbidden me to go walking alone. Rockets often flew over our heads when we went to school, but we hadn't gone to school for several days. One afternoon my Aunt Vathana, a young girl not yet eighteen, came to get me for a motorbike ride. I always enjoyed going off with her; the tree-lined avenues gave us the illusion of being out in the country. We were approaching the Chinese hospital when the motorbike skidded, and I heard what sounded like a tire bursting. My aunt stopped short. Sitting behind her sidesaddle on the bike, I clung tightly to her belt, listening to the whistle of the shells. A man on a bicycle went past us, and I was stunned to see that he was still pedaling even though his head had been blown off! His bike crashed into the closed front gate of a high school, the Lycée du 18-Mars. A few people were sprawled on the sidewalk, and we could hear the sirens of several ambulances. We ran home terror-stricken, dragging the motorbike with its flat tire. Vathana went home to her mother while I slipped quietly into my parents' house. My maternal grandmother lived next door to us with her two daughters, Vathana and my Aunt Nang, the mother of my cousin Tôn Ny, who would be so close to me in the months to come.

The next day was April 16, 1975, of evil memory: the heaviest shelling I remember, fires everywhere, the sky full of smoke, and explosions in every part of the city. My family—my parents, four daughters of whom I was the second oldest at twelve, and a little four-year-old brother—had been joined by the family of my Uncle Vong, whom we called Mitia Mir, with his wife, Nang, and their nine children: the oldest, Tôn Ny, was eleven, and the youngest, Sreï Peu, was eighteen months. We spent the day together in a deep trench that had been dug at the far end of the garden. Nearby my father and uncle buried a rifle and a pistol, family souvenirs that had never been used. I later learned that there had been a directive ordering everyone to hand in all weapons in their possession.

The next morning, everything was calm. No one dared to go out; we were waiting for something to happen. Suddenly we heard cheering and triumphant cries: "Kampuchea is free!" Through closed windows we saw the crowd of loiterers and homeless people who straggled around the city all day line up on both sides of the avenue, while down the center of the pavement, in single file, kids in black pants and jackets were marching, their guns on their shoulders, wearing sandals made out of pieces of tires. Without a word or a smile, they stared straight ahead. They were heading toward the center of the city. My sister pointed out to me a jeep at the head of the line, with a white flag flying over it. My father and uncle rushed to tear up a sheet, making a white flag that they hung from the window. To go out into the street, they changed from their overly "bourgeois" trousers into a cloth they wrapped around their hips, Gandhi-style. Was that what liberation was all about? Suddenly I heard them run back inside and rummage through the bathroom for a large towel—a red one. "The red flag is up; we have to have a red flag or they'll ransack the house!" The kid soldiers didn't look as if they wanted to loot anything; they just kept coming on silently, without looking at anything or anybody.[5]

SEVEN

POLITICS

SINIBALDI This is the final discussion in our series about Natalia Ginzburg, and it centers on her relationship with politics. Ginzburg is a member of Parliament, elected by two legislatures as an independent in the Communist Party.[1] But the subject also interests us because it confronts a broader theme—Ginzburg's relationship with her own times, with its problems and conflicts—which has come into play in all our discussions with her. We'll start with a reading of "An Invisible Government" (included in the collection *Imaginary Life*), written in June 1972, which we will discuss then with the author and with a guest, Vittorio Foa. But first let's listen to "An Invisible Govermnent":

Although I know nothing about politics, I am sometimes overcome with loathing, contempt, or with feelings of support and a passion for political events. These events, however, do not appear to me as a coherent picture, brightly and uniformly lit. They always appear like shreds or stumps or splinters onto which I cling like someone lost without a boat in the middle of a fast-flowing river.

One of the very few political ideas, perhaps the only one, I hold onto was handed to me when I was seven years old. It was explained to me what Socialism was, that is, I was told that it was equality of goods and equality of rights for all. It seemed to me to be something that should be done right away. I thought it odd that it hadn't already. I remember exactly the time and the room in which this phrase, which seemed to me to be so blatantly obvious and indispensable, was given to me. And even today it has the power to spark a kind of fire in me. Even today I marvel at the fact that this thing, that is, equality of goods and rights, has not been achieved and that it seems so complex and difficult to implement.

When I have to vote, I obey emotional impulses, and the sensation I have is a uniquely emotional one, as if I have to shake hands with a party and kiss it on both cheeks. This is certainly not how one should vote, I know. Every time I am given some instructions, I throw them away in the street and follow only instincts of irrational sympathies and affections. I am not able to vote with resignation, and I love the party for whom I will vote. When I go to vote, the memory of the only rudimentary political notion that I possess, that is, equality of goods and rights among men, is reawakened. I would like to know with absolute certainty who wants this, but because the explanations I get are conflicting and confused, I vote with my heart and blindly.

People I know and respect have said to me at times that if equality of goods and rights were to be achieved, I would lose a part of my freedom, I would not write anything else, and I would be horribly unhappy. The reason for this being that equality does not fall down from the sky but requires some subtle and terrible maneuvering. And it's true that I, too, believe that if I could no longer write, I would be very unhappy and perhaps would throw myself under a train. But I think that our personal happiness or unhappiness should not guide us in our political choices. What is lovely and pleasant for oneself is not necessarily lovely and pleasant for others. We wish for a better world, but it may be that in this better world there is no room for our own person. However, it is also possible to look at one's own destiny with indifference. I'm not sure if this is a political way of reasoning, that is, the kind that politicians accept. It is the way of reasoning of despairing people. I'm not sure there's room in politics for despairing people. I've a feeling there isn't.

SINIBALDI So then, Vittorio Foa, what do you say about this small political manifesto of Natalia Ginzburg's? Is there room in politics for "despairing people"?

VITTORIO FOA Of course, why shouldn't there be? If there weren't, Natalia wouldn't have gone into government. If she went into government, it means she thinks something can be done. And for whom should it be done? For those who despair, and even for those who still hope. They might be badly off, unhappy, alienated, excluded, but they haven't given up hope, which is why I think that when Natalia talks of despairing people, she is talking about a social and personal unhappiness. That is, Natalia quite rightly doesn't see the whole reality of society as existing in the collective sphere. She thinks we must also serve to alleviate the illness, the suffering, the desperate needs of each individual. Unhappiness can be collective; it can also be individual. It can be predicated on the inequalities and injustices in which we are immersed. It can also be predicated on personal circumstances. It seems to me that Natalia, in her work, in her life, has always been concerned with the pain of others. And she doesn't endorse despair; she promotes hope. That's how I've known her.

SINIBALDI Let's explain that Vittorio Foa is so important to any discussion of Natalia Ginzburg and politics because of their longstanding friendship. The readers of The Things We Used to Say will remember that Vittorio Foa was one of those familiar figures from Natalia's childhood who walked along the streets of Turin with her brothers and who they suddenly discovered had been plotting against the Fascists and then off to prison he went. At that point he became one of the distant, unreachable figures populating the young Natalia's imagination. But on the matter of politics, Vittorio Foa is important because from the vantage point of his political experience he differs from others in his reaction to Ginzburg's statement-cum-manifesto, "I know nothing about politics." Most of Ginzburg's friends see the statement as either a whimsical remark or a way to shield herself. So naturally they respond with, "It's true you know nothing about politics, so don't get involved," as she says her children said to her, or with, "No, you do know about politics, you can do all this." Vittorio Foa, conversely, has told Ginzburg, "It is precisely because you don't know anything about politics that you must get involved in it." So, what did you mean, Vittorio Foa, with this piece of advice? You wrote that Natalia Ginzburg would be a good politician.

FOA It's true she's a good politician, even if she understands nothing about politics. And in fact, what does it mean, not to understand anything about politics? . . . I believe that in politics there are various levels: one is utilitarian, which I don't judge as vulgar; it's necessary. But if you stay there, you don't use your imagination. And then you obstruct the movement of life and of political life itself. Then there's the ethical level, where things are done out of a sense of collectivity, with regard for others . . . and as far as these others go, you have to make a choice. For which others? Surely the ones who are oppressed by life, oppressed by circumstances. And finally there's the level of poetry, you see? Of imagination. These levels are not isolated. They often overlap. On the poetic level there's certainly an element of ethics. My feeling is that Natalia's politics exist at the ethical and poetic levels. In 1986, or thereabouts, together with Laura Balbo, a friend and colleague of Natalia's at the Chamber, we collected some short articles into a volume with this basic theme: what do we expect from the Communist Party? It was a little book entitled *Lettere da vicino* (Letters from nearby) and published by Einaudi, I think, in '86. Natalia's piece is interesting to read.

SINIBALDI Yes, we'll read it in just a moment. I wanted to ask Natalia what she thinks of Vittorio's definition of politics. She's always intimidated at first when people talk about politics.

NATALIA GINZBURG It's certainly true, yes.

SINIBALDI It's the remnant of a timidity that must go back to the 1930s, when Foa seemed distant and unreachable, in prison. Now fortunately he isn't in prison, and he certainly isn't unreachable and distant. I don't think Natalia need fear running into criticism from Vittorio Foa.

GINZBURG Actually, I'd like to say that many years ago, when the election was held for the president of the republic (in which Pertini won), *La Stampa* asked who should be elected. In response, I wrote "Terracini or Vittorio Foa." Terracini wrote me a lovely thank-you letter, whereas Vittorio . . .

FOA Gosh, didn't I thank you?

GINZBURG No.

FOA [*He laughs*] Really?

GINZBURG I got this really nice letter from Terracini, but nothing from you. But, be that as it may, I understand there's a utilitarian politics and an ethical one. Poetic politics I don't quite understand.

FOA It's about imagination. The use of imagination.

GINZBURG Imagination . . . I'm not sure . . .

FOA It's the capacity to choose things in life according to a certain criterion dictated by yourself, do you see? That is, you don't follow any prescribed rules. You make them up like you make up a poem. I'm not an expert on literature, but I think this is the poetic category. Or am I wrong?

GINZBURG In Parliament there are people I really like, and I like to imitate them, follow them. They are generally women. One is Livia Turco, whom I've mentioned before. My impression is that women in Parliament are more passionate than men. The men tend to be rather indifferent. And there are lots of women I like: one is Edda Fagni, one is Leda Colombini. They're brilliant, extraordinary. Livia Turco is very different from me because she sees everything from the woman's angle, and, well, when I went into government, they said to me I shouldn't go, my children especially. One of my sons said, "You'll be bored out of your mind because you won't understand anything." And it's true, I hardly ever understand anything, but I must say I don't get bored. I may be sitting there thinking my own thoughts, but every now and then I'll pick something up, which I take home and think about. Maybe I'll write an article, because I rarely give speeches.

FOA Can I ask you something, Natalia, which doesn't in fact directly involve politics? Talking about boredom and enjoyment—this program, do you like it?

GINZBURG Very much so.

FOA And you are enjoying yourself, inside as well?

GINZBURG I'm having a great time.

FOA Does it give you satisfaction?

GINZBURG It's very entertaining. It's just that I feel intensely narcissistic. But apart from that, I've enjoyed it very much.

FOA There's something I once realized, that I really like radio more than television. The public is there even when you can't see them, and so you have a rapport . . . It's a continuous exchange.

GINZBURG As when you write. You may not see the public, but they're there with you.

FOA You have that exchange. This is something worth thinking about, because it doesn't generally get discussed, does it?

SINIBALDI So, Vittorio Foa is doing a kind of analysis of what it feels like to be here.

FOA I added that because it was also my way of saying thank-you for doing this program.

SINIBALDI But, as far as Natalia Ginzburg is concerned, she is used to an invisible public in her work as a writer. Whereas in politics the public is visible, isn't that so, Natalia?

GINZBURG I'm not keen on the visible public, which is why I've made very few speeches. Very few.

SINIBALDI What was the subject of these speeches in the Chamber?

GINZBURG I don't remember them all. Once I spoke on sexual violence; once on disarmament; once on housing. And once, when it was still permitted to talk at length about whatever you liked, I talked about the rural communities that are no more, the rural way of life. This got me the response, "Well, once there were rural communities and there was pellagra!"[2] They threw this pellagra at me . . . but you can cure it, you can get rid of pellagra!

FOA It was brought on by a lifestyle of poverty.

GINZBURG And you can eliminate such lifestyles!

FOA Natalia has an elderly brother who's 90, Gino Martinoli. He's a great character, he's such an intelligent man. When Natalia made that particular speech in the Chamber, he wrote me a long letter, saying, "Seeing as you're a good friend of Natalia's, please explain to her that fortunately the world has changed. Yes, because if you knew what poverty there was then, how much unhappiness there was." So, on this point, there's disagreement between Natalia and me.

GINZBURG Profound disagreement.

FOA Well, not so much profound—because it may not be so profound—but constant.

[*Laughter*]

GINZBURG But the problem of poverty can be solved. Can't it?

SINIBALDI Natalia maintains that you can eradicate poverty without wiping out . . . rural life and a culture whose loss is felt like a wound in our culture as a whole—just as Pasolini saw it.

GINZBURG Pasolini said it as well, you see! It wasn't just me.

FOA Yes. Well, it's the story of the glowworms, that they'd all died out. But then the glowworms came back, glowworms, that's the extraordinary thing.

GINZBURG I don't believe it.

FOA Didn't they come back?

SINIBALDI Glowworms still exist. I fear that even with the reappearance of glowworms, we don't have grounds for much optimism.

FOA Well, on this problem of a rural culture, we're going together on June 16 to Matera, to do something related to Carlo Levi. Levi was the poet of our rural culture, wasn't he? Poet and painter of our rural culture, and we all loved him for this. But that rural memory is almost gone, isn't it? When Levi was writing, our rural culture was in sharp decline . . . He wrote at a time when industrial society was steaming ahead with extraordinary force. So these writings were strongly nostalgic. This nostalgia has ended.

SINIBALDI You mean we've lost the nostalgia as well?

FOA Not exactly. What I mean is I believe that nostalgia for the rural world could exist so long as there was the full strength of industrial society. Nowadays industrial society is in crisis, and soon we will have a literature of nostalgia for the culture of the worker, for industrial culture. But rural nostalgia is related to our grandparents' time. It's more remote. Don't you think so?

SINIBALDI That is, Vittorio Foa thinks that literature is like the owl of Minerva, that when the phenomenon, the culture, declines, literature takes it over in a nostalgic way as if to keep the memory of it alive.

GINZBURG There are, for example, wonderful things written by Parise that lament a world that no longer exists: those stories called *Solitudes*. Nostalgia is creative. The word has been discredited, but it is in fact a noble, creative word.

183

SINIBALDI And decisive for literature, don't you think?

GINZBURG For literature, yes.

FOA But look at this moment, when you're here also as a politician—don't you think that nostalgia is also very important for politics? In my opinion nostalgia is a point of departure for the future. Nostalgia is not passive.

GINZBURG Do you think so?

FOA I'm convinced of it! And I've studied this very thing over a long period. Whenever nostalgia is at its strongest, it means I need to do something new.

GINZBURG Yes, something to do with life, not death.

FOA Yes, something vital. Don't you agree?

GINZBURG That's true. It has been mistaken for something about things that have died, and that's wrong.

FOA Totally wrong! It's a category that is absolutely about life. Nostalgia is truly wonderful so long as it is a nostalgia for the future.

GINZBURG So long as it is a nostalgia for the past, which we want to link up to a future time.

FOA Well put, well put. Well, mine was the shorter version.

SINIBALDI You, Foa, defined political commitment and Natalia Ginzburg's Parliamentary work as a coherent extension of her creative work.

FOA When I read Natalia's novels there is an extraordinarily strong rapport between the continuity of daily life—with its tiny details, its tediousness, its little unhappinesses—and the tragic interruptions. Do you agree? Between the detail of life and the epic, or the tragedy of history? In Natalia's novels the historical background of the most dramatic period of our collective life, '35 to '45, is always present. Even when she doesn't talk about it, we feel the presence of Turin, Ivrea, the Abruzzi, Rome. There is at once a background of daily life and a tragic background. It seems to me that in her political work, in her apparent interest in tiny details, what we really see is this relationship with things that are common to everyone, with the things of time, including future time. So when in '83 the Communist Party asked Natalia to join its list of candidates, I knew straightaway that it wouldn't be like it usually was: that is, the well-known intellectual is called in to add luster to a list, make it look more honorable. No, I knew with Natalia it would be different, that she would bring to the vocation a real political content. It marked a change in politics . . . Natalia pays attention to the person and not purely to the political machine. Politics is a machine, that's a fact; but inside the machine, there is the person. It's very difficult to pay attention to the person. It seems to me that Natalia's politics are like this.

SINIBALDI Natalia, do you recognize yourself in this image of Vittorio Foa's? He once wrote, "morality versus technique."

FOA Yes, yes, morality versus technique.

GINZBURG I'd be happy if that were the case, though I'm not sure. I thought two things when they asked me to become a member of Parliament. I thought that it was something that was not at all my kind of thing, but I thought that as I had some fame as a writer (at the time I had won a prize, I'd written *The Manzoni Family*), perhaps I could be useful to the Communist Party. Then . . . I thought, "Who knows? I might actually be able to do something."

FOA But the things I'm describing very often don't involve awareness, you know? They go on independently of people being aware of them. I'm not describing Natalia's awareness, you see?

SINIBALDI [*He laughs*] . . . but the effect.

FOA Yes.

GINZBURG Sometimes when I'm there in Parliament, on that sofa in the corridor, I'm thinking deeply about things I want to write. It's not an unpleasant sensation; it comes over me like a spirit of contradiction, making me think of things that are the opposite of what is placed before me. In fact, they said to me, "One day you'll write a novel that will have the Chamber in it." I'll never write such a novel.

SINIBALDI "Novel fodder, here you'll find novel fodder," that's what they said to you.

GINZBURG Yes. But in fact I will never write a novel about that because there are things that just can't be put into my novels. But I do fish for things there. I might notice a profile, someone's nose. I might hear someone saying he's bought a car, and I put it into my book. I once put in a car that Rodotà had bought. He had bought a Ritmo, and I put a Ritmo into a novel. Not Rodotà, but his car.

SINIBALDI This is an unusual example of using the institution for one's own ends.

GINZBURG Perhaps I said something I shouldn't have.

SINIBALDI [*He laughs*] Not at all!

GINZBURG But you're sitting there and different thoughts come into your head.

SINIBALDI I'm sure it happens to everyone.

GINZBURG One thing I thought was that I had to be careful not to become somebody else. That I had to be very careful not to adopt a "physiognomy" different from the one I had.

SINIBALDI I think that's a danger you successfully avoided. In these last twenty or so minutes I'd like to touch on something that divides you two. It's a problem that we'll introduce via another extract, one Vittorio Foa mentioned a while ago, "Arabeschi" (Arabesques), which was included in the collection *Lettere da vicino* (Letters from close by), a book edited by Laura Balbo and Vittorio Foa and dedicated to a possible reinvention of the Left. It introduces the theme of Natalia Ginzburg's relationship with political parties, and with the Communist Party in particular, a subject of controversy between her and Vittorio Foa:

The Communist Party is often accused of not being red anymore but gray, that is, austere and frigid. So as not to appear too gray, it sometimes tries to put on showy colors, to imitate gestures and attitudes that it thinks will please the crowd. At such times the

Communist Party seems like a crow that is putting on peacock's feathers. Much better if it stays a crow. Those who believe in it are indifferent to the fact that it looks austere and gray: they want it to be absolutely sincere. They wouldn't want it to be frigid, but they are aware that frigidity doesn't melt so easily. You might say that for a political party, the consent and the approval of the crowd is of essential importance. That's true, but for the Communist Party, the consent and approval of the crowd cannot be curried through instruments or costumes that do not reflect its true nature. Those who trust in it want above all for it to be truthful and to scorn any kind of pretence. The Communist Party is also accused of being old; I think this accusation troubles it, and it tries too hard to seem young. But I think it should be proud of its old age: I think that for a party, as for a human being, youth blossoms in the old when it doesn't think about itself or wonder whether it is old or young. Old, in the Communist Party, is the idea that the working classes are still the most important thing. I think that here it should come up-to-date: the old social classes have changed and the old social order has been completely shattered and overturned. The exploited and persecuted are everywhere: The party's objective is therefore to seek them out and to get behind them.

I would like to see the Communist Party participate in government, but I would like it to do so without ever becoming a government party. I would like it to participate in government not with the characteristics of the winners but with those of the losers. I would like it to manage to govern without ever losing the supreme good of uncertainty and fragility. People will argue that in this way governments don't survive even for a day. And yet it must be possible to conceive of a force that rejects power; it must be possible to conceive of a force that rejects the optimistic characteristics of victory and maintains, in victory, the pessimism of the defeated. A force that keeps alive the memory of persecutions seen and lived through and detests force above all else. If it were to assume power, the Communist Party would not be gray anymore but would dress itself in all the colors of the rainbow: it would be open to all, and there would be room in it for everybody. It would be surrounded by every type of bird: crows, peacocks, sparrows, nightingales, and geese. It would not need to take on any particular appearance in order to please people; although bitter and full of doubt and uncertain in its spirit, it would also be utterly at peace. So much

so that soon people would stop thinking about it, would stop real-
izing it was there. People will say that the Communist Party is not
like this in any part of the world. It doesn't matter: there must still
be the possiblity of it being like this. And if there is this possiblity,
no matter how evanescent and unlikely, to picture a world made
up in this way is legitimate, at worst, useless. It is perhaps like
drawing arabesques across a wall. But I think that everyone, from
time to time, pictures a world governed in the way they would
like; I think that everyone, from time to time, starts drawing an
arabesque or two across a wall.

SINIBALDI There are many things about which you, Vittorio Foa and
Natalia Ginzburg, agree, but also many things about which you dis-
agree . . . for one, the change in the Communist Party . . . its change
of name and of tradition, the change in identity of this party.[3] Vittorio
Foa favors, Natalia Ginzburg rejects this process.

FOA These days the business of pro or con is not so important. I
don't think it interests anyone, just as I don't think anyone is really
interested in the fact that Natalia believed for a time that it was important for the Communist Party to know what it was. The important
thing with the Communist Party is to know what is useful to the people, not what is useful to it. As for its identity, nobody gives a damn
about it. Really—because your identity is simply what you are as you
move through a life that is changing. It's not something you have to
jealously guard. What is really at stake is a party's policy. I believe that's
what Natalia was saying in that piece, and she said something I like
very much: that we must go to government like losers, that victory
as destruction of the other is unacceptable. You can't think in terms
of destroying the other: if I win, I must be aware that the other one is
always present. If I make a choice between two different suggestions,
and I choose A instead of B, I don't eradicate B; B exists. This is the
new way of doing politics, which is what Natalia was asking for. But
this way of doing politics, never to eradicate the other, not to have an
idea of power that is exclusive and therefore destructive, this is a key
step. It is a cultural stance that emerged in the eighties—those same
eighties that were dismissed as awful compared with the wonderful
seventies, which ironically saw the slow, daily decline of the Left. In
the 1980s, in the middle of so many defeats, we see, all the same, the
emergence of different cultures—the culture of the environment, the
culture of rights, women's culture . . . a pluralism that allows you to

187

know you aren't at the center of the world, you aren't the world's navel; that others have equal rights . . . sorry?

SINIBALDI No, no, carry on, Vittorio. I just wanted Natalia to have the right to reply [*he laughs*], to put her own view across.

GINZBURG No, no, on this we totally agree, there's no doubt. But as for what you said before, that the Communist Party can forget about its own identity. I don't agree: no one must lose their own identity. One's identity, one's memories, one's roots . . . these must be preserved. So in renewing the Communist Party I would like its identity, its physiognomy, to remain intact. For example, its members who have maybe made mistakes but who are its memory. I'm not thinking of Stalin. Stalin committed crimes, and we perhaps understood this too late. Recently when I read the letters of Tsvetaeva, I saw what a terrible country the Soviet Union was. And then I read the memoirs of Bukharin's widow: these books had an enormous impact on me. Tragic; a tragic reality. But I mean that we, in Italy, have other memories, different ones, cherished ones. Berlinguer, for instance, I used to love him a great deal. I went into government partly because Berlinguer was there at the time. Maybe he made mistakes, but so what? A politician always makes mistakes, if he's in power, with a huge burden of responsibility on his shoulders, a man makes mistakes. And perhaps Berlinguer made mistakes, but for me he was an extraordinary man. Gorbachev, too, is an extraordinary man. He may also have made mistakes, but he's the greatest politician, I think, of our century. And last night I heard a program of Vittorio Strada's who said of Gorbachev, "But there's no real thought in him." What does he mean, no thought? His thoughts are truly great. For me Gorbachev is the hope of this time. We were talking earlier about hope. For me, Gorbachev is hope.

SINIBALDI Vittorio Foa, apart from the appreciations of Gorbachev, how can we resolve . . . ?

FOA No, no, on the contrary. On the subject of Gorbachev we are very much in agreement. Even if he is one of these losers, just as Natalia wishes, it's true, he's the greatest of men.

SINIBALDI And this problem of identity Natalia mentioned before, how can it be resolved?

FOA In a very easy way: this party doesn't exist to give identity to its members. This is a problem of alarming egotism, that the party must offer peace of mind. The party must serve the people, that's its role.

188

GINZBURG I didn't say look after the peace of mind of its members! But it should conserve its physiognomy; in this way it serves the people by being itself, staying itself, not taking on different identities. Not allying itself with the Socialists.

FOA [*He laughs*] Well, on that last point I totally agree! But I meant something else. The disagreement I have with Natalia is not over this issue. It's over a much more important one: how we judge life. Is life beautiful or ugly? This is what we argue over continually.

SINIBALDI Right, we have very little time left, but I would like to hear where you both stand on this.

GINZBURG Awful, that's what life is!

FOA I think there are two sides to life: an ugly one, or an awful one as she puts it—think of organized crime, crime that thrives within politics, rich people who don't pay their taxes, a long list of awful things—the ugliness keeps on growing. And the ugliest thing of all is resignation: to accept these things This is the greatest evil of our time, surely. But this is only one side of life: then there is the other side in which our energies and our hopes grow. In different forms from past ones, not according to tradition, but it happens. The city of Fiuggi sends its mafia-style godfather packing via four days of demonstrations in front of the town hall, and the godfather is the political son of Andreotti, for instance. These things happen: near the city of Massa they close a factory even though the workers (the bosses, above all) want to keep it open. Leoluca Orlando wins 70,000 votes over Andreotti, Craxi, and Forlani together, that is, a triumph against the power structure. We see the awful side, and we see the side of hope.

GINZBURG Well, Leoluca Orlando I agree with.

SINIBALDI This is Vittorio's vision of the world, summed up in just a few seconds, brilliantly done.

GINZBURG But then you have the fear that Leoluca Orlando will be pushed to one side.

SINIBALDI And that Gorbachev—

GINZBURG —that Gorbachev won't make it.[4] Yes, it's difficult to hope. I understand that it's right to hope, but I don't see how.

SINIBALDI But do you envy Vittorio Foa for his hope, or do you think he is superficial because he has hope?

GINZBURG No, I don't think he's superficial. He's an optimist.

SINIBALDI You say the word "optimist" with a note of disdain.

189

FOA It's the famous fool's optimism. [*He laughs*]

GINZBURG I don't disdain him, but I find him optimistic, and I am unable to see some of these things as containing a seed of hope. Of course let's wish for things; but what I admire is courage. I admire courage in people. The judge Carlo Palermo had great courage. I had the great joy to vote for him.

SINIBALDI So, Vittorio, Natalia says that you are an optimist. Is Natalia a pessimist, in your opinion? Is this what is wrong?

FOA I think so, I think so. I have always wondered about Natalia. She is sad. In her books she is sad. In her person, in her relationships with friends, she is sad. There is a lot that is charming in this sadness. But it isn't borne of life's events: it is inside of her. That's it. When I read what she writes, at a certain point I ask myself, what is this internal sadness of hers? I know I can't explain it, so I just give in to the joy of reading her. And it was like this even when she was fourteen, when I met her.

GINZBURG Yes, that maybe is true. But I do sometimes see the funny side of things. I'd like to point that out.

FOA A sense of humor is not the opposite of sadness, though.

GINZBURG No, it isn't.

FOA No.

GINZBURG No. But when it comes to the things we write about there is the reflection of the outside; the life we have reflects on the things we write.

SINIBALDI Probably Vittorio Foa thinks that there is a prejudice, so to speak, in the way you look upon the world, there's a screen of pessimism and sadness. This is what, I think, he is accusing you of, in an affectionate and friendly way.

GINZBURG There may well be a black side to me, a melancholia that comes out in my books, but the world in which we live isn't happy.

SINIBALDI I don't think even Foa thinks that . . .

GINZBURG No, but he says that . . .

FOA But children are born. Children are born.

GINZBURG Yes, too many of them!

NOTES

CHAPTER ONE

1. Filippo Turati (1857–1932) had strong ties with European Socialism and played a key role in the creation in Italy of a political party for the working class. His importance as a figure who opposed Fascism led to his flight from Italy to Paris in 1926, from where he continued to support the anti-Fascist movement—*trans*.

2. For the English edition, see *The Things We Used to Say*, trans. and with an intro. by Judith Woolf (Manchester: Carcanet, 1997)—*trans*.

3. Ferruccio Parri (1890–1981) served as an official in the First World War and was decorated several times for his bravery. He became an active member of anti-Fascist intellectual circles, collaborating in the publication of the review *Caffè* and organizing the escape of persecuted fellow anti-Fascists. He was arrested in 1926 for his part in Turati's escape and had periods of imprisonment and political exile. He became a leader of Partito d'Azione and was later a senator—*trans*.

4. Carlo Rosselli (1899–1937) was one of the cofounders, along with his brother Nello Rossi and Salvemini, of the legendary anti-Fascist review, *Non mollare* and participated in the Turati escape. From 1927 he was sent into political exile on Lipari, but he escaped on a motorboat and went to Paris where he helped with the French side of the Justice and Liberty movement (see fn. 7). He was assassinated in France, along with his brother, on the orders of the Italian military espionage service—*trans*.

5. Alessandro ("Sandro") Pertini (1896–1990) was an active anti-Fascist in his youth and assisted in Turati's famous escape before being forced to flee

himself. Following his return to Italy in 1927, he was condemned to ten years in prison followed by a period of internment, which he endured until 1943 when he was released. After taking part in the battle against the Germans in Rome in that same year, he was arrested and condemned to death. He escaped from prison and went to the north of Italy to collaborate with revolutionary anti-Fascists. Following the war, several government appointments led to him being elected speaker of the Italian Parliament then, in 1978, president of the republic—*trans.*

6. Adriano Olivetti (1901–1960) studied in the United States before taking over the running of the family firm (the famous typewriter manufacturer) where he was successful in bringing in new marketing strategies that ensured that Olivetti became a household name. In addition to his entrepreneurial activities, he was involved in the early stages of the Einaudi publishing house and was a committed Socialist, becoming an MP in 1958—*trans.*

7. Justice and Liberty was the name of a clandestine organization and anti-Fascist political movement set up in Paris in 1929 by a group of political exiles. Its principles were opposed to a return to the power structures of the pre-Fascist era, advocating its own revolutionary program which it publicized via a series of journals. Dispersed in 1940 with the occupation of France, the movement then became part of Partito d'Azione (founded in 1942) which, as well as proposing a new form of liberal Socialism, was also actively involved in the partisan movement—*trans.*

8. Leone Ginzburg (1909–1944) whom Natalia married in 1938, came to Italy from Russia as a child. By his early twenties he was teaching Russian literature at Turin University before refusing to swear the oath of allegiance to Fascism and joining the Justice and Liberty movement (see n. 7). He was arrested in 1934 but returned to Turin after imprisonment where he and his friend, Giulio Einaudi, founded a new publishing house (Einaudi). From 1940 to 1943, as a result of his anti-Fascist tendencies, he, Natalia, and their two young children were sent into political exile in the Abruzzi region of Italy. While an internee he managed to maintain an involvement in the Einaudi publishing house and, once out of exile, became active again in politics. He was arrested in 1943 and died a few months later in Rome's Regina Coeli Prison—*trans.*

9. Vittorio Foa (born 1910) was a prominent anti-Fascist who took an active part in the Justice and Liberty movement. Arrested in 1935 and condemned to fifteen years of political exile, he later became a member of the resistance alongside fellow members of Partito d'Azione. From 1948 he devoted much time to union issues and remained a prominent member of the new Left—*trans.*

10. Giancarlo Pajetta (1911–1990) became a member of the Communist Party at the age of fourteen and was sent to prison for two years in 1927 for his anti-Fascist activities. On his return he was again a member of a

Communist clandestine group and spent a further ten years in prison. He subsequently became a member of Parliament and a high-profile member of the Communist Party on an international level—*trans*.

11. Luigi Salvatorelli (1886–1974) was a historian and journalist who was a fierce opponent of Fascism and subsequently a founder member of Partito d'Azione—*trans*.

12. Guglielmo Ferrero (1871–1943) was a sociologist who wrote a series of volumes on aspects of ancient Roman history, some of which earned him the censure of historians who found his approach to be flawed. An anti-Fascist, he fled to Switzerland in 1930 and remained there until his death, occupying various teaching posts in Geneva—*trans*.

13. Cesare Pavese (1908–1950) studied American literature and quickly became an established translator of such authors as Gertrude Stein, Daniel Defoe, and Charles Dickens as well as frequenting Turin intellectual circles along with Leone Ginzburg, Giulio Einaudi, and Vittorio Foa. His involvement in politics was less overt than other members of his circle, but he was nevertheless sent into political exile for one year and later became a crucial member of the editorial team at Einaudi. He wrote novels and poetry that, along with his diary *Il mestiere di vivere* (published posthumously), established him as one of Italy's better-known authors. A solitary man, he suffered from depression and several failed love affairs and, at the age of 42, took his own life in a hotel room in Turin—*trans*.

14. Giulio Einaudi (1912–1999) was the son of a well-known economist, Luigi Einaudi, who was to become, in 1948, president of Italy. Giulio founded the publishing house that was to bear his family name and was a member of a circle of friends who opposed Fascism—*trans*.

15. Felice Balbo (1914–1982) worked for the Einaudi publishing house from 1941. In his youth he rejected the values of his aristocratic, Catholic background and became an active member of the Christian Communist Party. His intellectual interests ranged from political ideology (Marxism and post-Marxism) to religion and philosophy; in 1952 he broke away from the Communist Party as he felt it was impossible for a Catholic to belong to a Marxist party. In later years he showed a continued interest in issues raised by the impact of industrialized society—*trans*.

16. Carlo Levi (1902–1975)-was one of Italy's internationally known writers because of the success of *Christ Stopped at Eboli*, his depiction of life in a town in Lucania where he was sent as a political exile because of his opposition to the Fascist regime. A founder member of the Justice and Liberty movement, he later fled to France, where he became a member of the Resistance. In 1963, he was elected to the Senate—*trans*.

17. Ernesto Rossi (1896–1967) was a key member of the Florentine anti-Fascist movement who was partly responsible for the publication, in 1925, of the clandestine journal *Non mollare*. A founder member of the Justice and

Liberty movement, he lived through imprisonment and exile before becoming a leader of Partito d'Azione. His writings express his opposition to economic domination and distortion by large public and private concerns and show how he was influenced by the theories of Luigi Einaudi (Giulio's father)—*trans*.

18. Riccardo Bauer (1896–1982) served in the First World War for which he was awarded the bronze medal. Bauer then completed a degree in Milan in economics. Aware of the importance of issues affecting workers' unions and concerned with the growing passivity among Fascist-influenced Italians, Bauer conceived of a new journal (*Caffè*), which became a major critique of Fascism. Despite periods of confinement and continued police surveillance, he was among the founder members of the Justice and Liberty movement in Milan. He later became a member of Partito d'Azione, which, however, he left as its ethos conflicted with his own liberal-democratic approach and broader humanitarian interests—*trans*.

19. She is referring to a discussion between Leone Ginzburg, Guido M. Gatti, and Alfredo Parente that took place over about a three-year period, from 1930 to 1933, in the pages of the journal *Rassegna musicale*. The subject of the debate was what significance was to be attributed to "interpretation": if it should be understood as merely the reproduction of written music, or instead as allowing for a degree of variation and freedom of expression on the part of the performer vis-à-vis the composer. See the anthology from *La rassegna musicale*, ed. Luigi Pestalozzi (Milan: Feltrinelli, 1966).

20. Piero Gobetti (1901–1926) was a writer and political activist. By the age of seventeen, he had founded his own journal, *Energie nuove*, which succeeded in publishing articles from a wide cross-section of intellectuals, including Croce and Gramsci. He was a promoter of the original ideals behind the Risorgimento, which he felt would only be realized if driven by secular interests and the needs of the proletariat. Fascism was viewed as a step backward and his uncompromising stance caused him to be persecuted and, finally, to escape to France. His ideas were absorbed into the anti-Fascist campaigns of the 1920s and beyond—*trans*.

21. The recording was part of a radio program called *Arti e scienze*, broadcast on 4 December 1950.

22. Natalia Ginzburg, "Ricordo di Carlo Levi," *Corriere della Sera*, 8 January 1975.

23. Cesare Garboli (1928–) is a renowned literary critic and the coeditor of the review *Paragone*. He has also translated Molière, Pinter, and Shakespeare. Other publications include the above-mentioned *Falbalas* (a collection of essays) and volumes on Pascoli and Soldati, which he edited—*trans*.

24. Eugenio Montale (1896–1981) was, as a young man, a member of the group of intellectuals who opposed Fascism, leading him to sign an anti-Fascist manifesto in 1925, the same year in which his first book of poetry

(*Cuttlefish Bones*) came out. He became a key figure in Florentine intellectual circles and survived the war years by working as a translator. He continued publishing poetry until, by the 1950s, he was considered Italy's leading living poet—*trans*.

25. Elio Vittorini (1908–66) was a novelist, translator, and literary critic. His novels, examples of the neorealism movement, dealt with Italy's experience of Fascism. With Pavese, he pioneered the translation into Italian of U.S. and English writers. The anti-Fascist novel *Conversations in Sicily* was first published in 1941. After the war, he published the political-cultural journal Il *Politecnico* (1945–47), and later, with Italo Calvino, edited the literary journal Il *Menabò*. He served as head of the foreign literature deparment at Einaudi—*trans*.

26. For an English translation, see "Portrait of a Writer," in *Never Must You Ask Me*, trans. with an intro. by Isabel Quigly (London: Joseph, 1973)—*trans*.

27. The speaker refers to events of 10 May 1990, when a group of neo-Nazis desecrated many tombs in the Jewish cemetery in Carpentras, France. The following day, further attacks on Jewish cemeteries took place, prompting a strong outcry throughout Europe against the beginnings of what seemed to be a new wave of anti-Semitic violence. Natalia Ginzburg wrote an article that came out in the review *Rinascita* entitled "Se vien meno la memoria" [Lest we forget], 27 May 1990, n. 16.

28. For an English translation, see *The Road to the City; and, The Dry Heart*, trans. Frances Frenaye (Manchester: Carcanet, 1989)—*trans*.

29. Velletri is an ancient town 39 kilometers south of Rome, which has a tradition for viticulture and livestock. Its proximity to the capital has turned it into an overflow for the city—*trans*.

30. Written by Erskine Caldwell, *Tobacco Road* appeared in 1932.

31. S. Benco, review of *La strada che va in città*, Il Piccolo, 30 July 1942.

32. For an English translation, see "Winter in the Abruzzi," in *The Little Virtues*, trans. Dick Davis (Manchester: Carcanet, 1985)—*trans*.

CHAPTER TWO

1. For an English translation, see "The Son of Man," in *The Little Virtues*, trans. Dick Davis (Manchester: Carcanet, 1985)—*trans*.

2. Originally founded in 1853 and driven by the struggle for republican unity, the party lost impetus until it was able to assist Garibaldi in the liberation of the south in 1860. It was revived in 1942, with former militant members of the Justice and Liberty movement and left-wing republicans at its core. Its goal was to achieve a new form of Socialism, responding to the genuine needs of the workers and bring about drastic reform to the social and economic structure of the country. It had its own anti-Fascist journal and, following the war, was briefly the governing party, but the conflicting beliefs and backgrounds of its members prevented it from becoming established—*trans*.

3. See chapter 1, n. 15—*trans*.

4. For an English translation, see "Two Communists," in *Never Must You Ask Me*, trans. with an intro. by Isabel Quigly (London: Joseph, 1973)—*trans*.

5. L. Ingrao, review of È *stato così*, in *Rinascita* 4, nos. 11–12 (Nov.—Dec., 1947): 352.

6. For an English translation, see *All Our Yesterdays*, trans. Angus Davidson (Manchester: Carcanet), 1985.

7. P. Citati, review of È *stato così*, in *Belfagor* 9, no. 3 (3 May 1953). [The author, Pietro Citati (b. 1930) was a literary critic for various newspapers. His publications include studies on Goethe, Manzoni, and Tolstoy—*trans*.]

8. Felice Balbo, *L'uomo senza miti* (Einaudi, 1945) was followed in 1946 by *Il laboratorio dell'uomo*.

9. N. Gallo, "L'ultima narrativa italiana," in *Società* 9, n. 3 (1953): 340–399.

10. In early 1982 the publishing house of Giulio Einaudi went into receivership, thus avoiding bankruptcy. The lawyer Giuseppe Rossotto was named as the receiver.

11. The original text contains an extract from Natalia Ginzburg's translation of Proust's *Swann's Way* as an example of her work as a Italian translator—*trans*.

12. N. Ginzburg, "Memoria contro Memoria," in *Paragone* 39, n. 462 (1988): 3–9.

13. *Giovine* is a more literary version of Ginzburg's word choice, *giovane*—*trans*.

14. Giulio Bollati was an editor at Einaudi—*trans*.

15. For an English translation, see "Portrait of a Friend," in *The Little Virtues*, trans. Dick Davis (Manchester: Carcanet, 1985)—*trans*.

16. This was a book series published by Einaudi with Vittorini as sponsoring editor that sought to give young writers a space in which to write about the problems and realities of contemporary life—*trans*.

17. Franco Venturi (1914–1994) was an anti-Fascist activist, member of the Justice and Liberty movement, and noted historian of European thought and Russia—*trans*.

18. Norberto Bobbio (1909–) taught philosophy of law at Turin University and became a member of the Italian Socialist Party. He has published extensively on matters of law, ethics, and politics and is a life senator—*trans*.

19. See n. 10 above.

CHAPTER THREE

1. For the English-language translation, see "My Vocation," in *The Little Virtues*, trans. Dick Davis (Manchester: Carcanet, 1985). The Italian title is "Il mio mestiere"—*trans*.

2. The title "My Vocation" could equally be translated as "My Job," which was possibly the sense in which Elsa Morante saw it and the reason she objected. See also "My Craft," in *A Place to Live*, trans. Lynne Sharon Schwartz (N.Y.: Seven Stories Press, 2002)—*trans.*

3. For the English-language translation, see *Voices in the Evening*, trans. D. M. Low (London: Hogarth Press, 1963)—*trans.*

4. L. Marchionne Picchione, *Natalia Ginzburg* (Florence: Nuova Italia, 1978).

5. E. Montale, "Lessico famigliare, crudele con dolcezza," in *Corriere della Sera*, 7 July 1963.

6. This was the name given to Drusilla Tanzi, Natalia Ginzburg's maternal aunt who later married Eugenio Montale.

7. G. Ferrata, "Ringraziamento a Natalia Ginzburg," in *Rinascita*, 27 April 1963.

8. C. Garboli, *Introduzione a Lessico famigliare* (Milan: Oscar Mondadori, 1972).

9. For an English translation, see *Dear Michael*, trans. Sheila Cudahy (London: Owen, 1975). The same translation was published in the United States under the title *No Way* (N.Y.: Harcourt Brace Jovanovich, 1973)—*trans.*

CHAPTER FIVE

1. See chapter 1, n. 27.

2. During the Olympics [in Munich], the Palestinian faction Black September killed fourteen Israeli athletes.

3. The poet Paul Celan, whose parents were deported in 1942, drowned himself in 1970 at the age of fifty. Bruno Bettelheim (1903–1990), after having been for one year in the Dachau and Buchenwald concentration camps, emigrated (in 1939) to the United States where he directed the University of Chicago's Sonia Shankman Orthogenic School. He took his own life in a rest home in Maryland. The Austrian writer Jean Améry (pseudonym of Hans Mayer, 1912–1978), having been a prisoner at Auschwitz for two years, committed suicide in Salzburg.

4. This was a conversation led by Alberto Gozzi broadcast in 1982 and reported in *Riga*, 13, devoted to Primo Levi.

CHAPTER SIX

1. For an English translation, see "My Vocation," in *The Little Virtues*, trans. Dick Davis (Manchester: Carcanet, 1985)—*trans.*

2. See Sandra Petrignani's interview of Natalia Ginzburg, published in the newspaper *Il Messaggero* on 22 February 1989, entitled "When the Critic Is a Traveling Companion." During the course of the interview Ginzburg again takes up the question introduced by Garboli, on the physicality of literature, and thus on the determination of a writer's sex, in terms much more pronounced than those in which the present text is formulated: "And then that

whole discussion on the masculine and feminine in my writing. It enlightened me; it made me see something in myself that I had not been aware of." The notion of the difference between the masculine and feminine now seems well on the way to taking shape. It should be noted that both the interview by Sandra Petrignani as well as the present text belong to the same period.

3. After the withdrawal of Vietnamese troops from Cambodia in 1988, the demand for a resolution on an international level led to the Paris accord in 1989, which set a timetable for a cease-fire by May 1992. But the fear of a possible return of the Khmer Rouge was still very strong.

4. Pol Pot died on 15 April 1998.

5. For an English translation, see Molyda Szymusiak, *The Stones Cry Out. A Cambodian Childhood, 1975–1980* (London: Cape, 1987)—*trans.*

CHAPTER SEVEN

1. During the ninth legislature, from 1984 to 1987, she was elected to represent Turin; and in the tenth, until her death in 1991, for Perugia.

2. Pellagra is a disease caused by dietary deficiencies and characterized by skin lesions and gastrointestinal and neurological disturbances—*trans.*

3. The allusion here is to the notable transformation of Italy's Communist Party into a democratic party of the Left. Ginzburg never looked favorably on this transformation.

4. It was the time of perestroika, the restructuring of the entire political, economic, and bureaucratic system of the Soviet Union that Gorbachev was pursuing. Things subsequently took a different path, and Gorbachev, just as Ginzburg feared, "didn't make it." He was the victim of a coup d'état organized by the right wing of the Communist Party, which opposed the renewal. Gorbachev was removed from power, the Soviet Union was dissolved, and with the support of the Pentagon and the U.S. Congress, Boris Yeltsin took control.

INDEX